Not Without Design

Not Without Design

by
MARVIN J. ROSENTHAL

THE FRIENDS OF ISRAEL
Gospel Ministry, Inc.
West Collingswood, New Jersey

NOT WITHOUT DESIGN

The Friends of Israel Gospel Ministry, Inc.
P. O. Box 123
West Collingswood, N.J. 08107

First Edition 1980

Printed in the United States of America
Library of Congress Catalog Number 80-81031
ISBN 0-915540-27-4

Foreword

Realism, by simple definition, is facing facts as they are. The problem is, facts are often disturbing, disheartening or downright frightening. To a world in which evil is proliferating at a velocity roughly equivalent to the speed of light, facing up to reality is not a pleasant exercise. Consequently, millions of people choose to ignore, deny or flee from the somber realities assailing the world in our lifetime. Liberal religionists attempt to soothe us by insisting that man isn't really so bad after all. Political opportunists, on the other hand, shout that the system can be saved, if we will appoint their persons and parties as exclusive salvagers. Cultists retreat into the phantom revelations of satanically deluded people seeking to find rest without repentance. Still others shriek above the flashing lights and pulsating discord for people to find release in lives divorced from any semblance of moral restraint. These are all futile enterprises. Refusing to deal with reality will not force it to turn from one's door. Sooner or later, it must be reckoned with.

In the book you hold in your hand, Marv Rosenthal forthrightly addresses the vital questions bound up in the stern realities now facing mankind. His is not, however, a realism that will lead you to the brink of despair. On the contrary, it is a realism which is carefully woven into the rich tapestry of divine optimism. **Not Without Design** objectively appraises the problems confronting us, but then moves far beyond to project above the stage of earth's seemingly chaotic patchwork the crystal image of a divine design — one of consummate symmetry that touches every area of man's experience and destiny. The author states and substantiates through a skillfully selected compilation of biblical references, that God has a design for mankind; a design for a redeemer; a design for Israel; a design for these last days in which we now move; and, surpassingly, a design for eternity.

In the years of our close association and friendship, I have been repeatedly impressed by Marvin's ability to grasp the essence of a truth or historical situation and then communicate it in contemporary terms one can easily understand and identify with. This is precisely what he has done in this work. There is a refreshing crispness about it. The book is theologically sound, but totally devoid of the tedious elements so often found in books of this kind. **Not Without Design** is concise, yet satisfyingly broad in scope, detail and illustration.

In short, the book will leave the believer securely resting in the Blessed Hope and rejoicing in the glory of God, while the unbeliever will find a clear case for receiving Jesus Christ as Saviour and Sovereign of his life.

— Elwood McQuaid

Acknowledgments

NOT WITHOUT DESIGN was written amidst the pressure of an exciting, full-orbed ministry. It was the author's desire to give to the Lord a "special" love gift — that is, to do some "tent making". Consequently, portions of the manuscript were written in motel rooms where preaching assignments brought him, or high in the clouds perched in the body of a soaring jet, and not too infrequently in his study at home long after the clock had struck midnight.

But, that it has been written at all is to acknowledge indebtedness to others. A co-worker and friend, Amy Julian, typed and retyped the rough drafts. My secretary, Margie Whittley, read the manuscript and made helpful suggestions. Esteemed colleagues, Will Varner, my brother Stan Rosenthal, and Elwood McQuaid, interacted with the manuscript's emphasis and nuances of theology, the latter graciously consenting to write the foreword. Tom Allen used his dedicated art ability to help design the cover. Carol Slimm rushed the typesetting of the final manuscript to completion to meet a pressing deadline. And my good friend and associate, Ray Oram, handled all the details of seeing the book through printing and publication.

Not to be overlooked is my eleven-year-old son, David, who willingly gave up some wrestling matches and bowling outings with his dad to provide some extra time for writing.

Finally, a word of appreciation must be expressed to my beloved wife, Marbeth, who encouraged me to undertake the project. She read the manuscript and made valuable suggestions related to content and style. But more than that, though my ministry often takes me away from home far more than either of us would choose, she saw this additional endeavor not as an intrusion into our already limited time together, but as an occasion for joint further ministry. At a time when the world spurns the traditional and biblical role of the woman as a helpmeet to her husband, she has carried that mantle with dignity and distinction, for which I shall be eternally grateful.

Dedication

NOT WITHOUT DESIGN is dedicated to a select group of missionary-minded churches and committed, godly believers. Through their prayers, encouragement and gifts, they have helped sustain the worldwide evangelistic outreach of The Friends of Israel Gospel Ministry for forty-two years. Some of these churches and friends are known to the author. I delight in the fact that all are known to God.

Table of Contents

Introduction

Let me say it right up front and without apology — the world is in a mess, and it's a big one! If the planet Earth were a volcano, an eruption would be imminent. If the Earth were a giant meteor, it would be plummeting at break-neck speed toward collision. If the Earth were the sun, it would be setting, not to prepare for a new day, but to end an age whose foundations have been eroded. If the Earth were Humpty Dumpty, it would be ready to fall, and all the king's horses and all the king's men wouldn't be able to put the planet Earth back together again (only God's Son will be capable of that feat).

The insanity of the present hour has reached epidemic proportions. Not only does twentieth-century man not have the right answers to pressing, critical problems, he's so far off center that he doesn't even have the right questions.

Mankind has traded God's eternal principles for temporal, secular humanism with disastrous consequences.

These are not, I think, the words of a pessimist but of a biblical realist. Nor does what is happening in today's world surprise the student of God's Word. The cause, course and consummation of human history are clearly revealed in the Bible — God has given to man a blueprint. History is NOT WITHOUT DESIGN, and that design indicates that God has not called His servants to salvage a lost world but, rather, to preach a saving Gospel to lost men.

Like the mighty current of the ocean, man can choose to try to swim against the divine plan and perish against the rocks and shoals, or submit to it and be gently carried into the harbor of peace, security and endless life.

Marv Rosenthal
International Director
The Friends of Israel Gospel Ministry, Inc.

Every crushed heart, every broken body, every disturbed mind — the collective tears of the human race can trace their roots back to the sin of Adam and Eve in the Garden of Eden.

1

In His Image

And God said, Let us make man in our image, after our likeness; and let them have dominion over the fish of the sea, and over the fowl of the air, and over the cattle, and over all the earth, and over every creeping thing that creepeth upon the earth. So God created man in his own image, in the image of God created he him; male and female created he them.

Genesis 1:26-27

The climactic crowning act of God in creation was the creation of man. Created last in time, he was first in importance. To man was given the divine right to be king of the earth. He was to have dominion — to give names to the animal creation — to rule and reign.

From among all of creation, only Adam and Eve were fashioned in the image and likeness of God. That is, they possessed mind, heart and will — intellectual capability, emotional capability and volitional capability. Adam and Eve could think God's thoughts after Him, respond to God's love and do God's bidding. The potential for an intimate, satisfying, eternal relationship with God, the Potter, was fashioned into the bosom of man, the clay. He was created to proclaim with his mouth and demonstrate with his life the intrinsic, eternal perfections of God and to enjoy Him forever.

It is in that solitary fact that man is set apart from and infinitely higher than the animal creation. It is that same fact which gives to mankind its dignity, nobility and worth. Animals can think, feel and do. Like man, they possess intellectual, emotional and volitional capability, but that capability can only be exercised with great limitation horizontally toward the finite world. It cannot be exercised vertically toward the infinite God.

Since mankind was created with the potential for a perfect and eternal relationship with God, the worth and dignity of man can only be understood to the degree that the greatness of God is comprehended. The psalmist said:

By the word of the Lord were the heavens made, and all the host of them by the breath of his mouth. He gathereth the waters of the sea together as an heap; he layeth up the depth in storehouses. Let all the earth fear the Lord; let all the inhabitants of the world stand in awe of him. For he spoke, and it was done; he commanded, and it stood fast.
Psalm 33:6-9

Put negatively, if God is relegated to the position of being an opiate for the masses, if belief in a Creator is scoffed at as being the result of blind, unreasonable and unreasoning faith, if man is simply the product of billions of years of evolution beginning with some unknown gasses or primeval slime and mud, then man is not to be significantly distinguished from the animal world from which he supposedly sprang and life loses purpose and worth.

So why not war? What's a few hundred million lives, more or less, in this overpopulated world of four billion?

Let the bombs fall! And why not drugs? How important is it that a mind is blown and a body ruined? And why not a physical crime? What's the big deal if a man is killed or a woman violated? And why not a permissive society? After all, if there is no eternal God, surely there are no eternal principles of morality. And why not corrupt government and self-seeking politicians, many of whose primary concern is to perpetuate their power and longevity? Never mind that millions of people are "ripped off". And why not a terminated pregnancy? Who's really hurt if an unwanted child is never born? If man is not to be distinguished from the animal, why not live like the animal?

And that's right where twentieth-century man is at. He's lost his way and life is dirt cheap. He's like a blind man in a dark room looking for a black cat that isn't there, and unless man realizes that he was created in the image of God, that he is an everlasting being, that he is accountable to his Creator, he will continue to sail his broken craft on a sea of despair and hopelessness, often unwilling to admit that he has no map or compass for the journey. His heart will continue to itch, but he won't know how to scratch it.

And the enormity of man's need is only heightened by the reality that a sure remedy is available — available to all — free of charge, his for the reaching out and taking. But, with limited exceptions, most refuse to break the chains of pride that bind them and acknowledge accountability to a higher Being. In the words of a popular song, they go through life singing, "I did it my way!", without giving thought to the fact that if God should withhold the ability to breathe for a few minutes, they would fall prone on their faces — dead!

But, make no mistake about it, humanity's dilemma

is of its own making. Mankind is not a super-sophisticated computer that can only print out what was programmed in. Having created man in His own image with the ability to choose, God gave to man a choice. The one tree in the midst of the garden — the tree of the knowledge of good and evil — was not to be eaten. Disobedience would bring death. To the first man and woman God said:

Do you understand with your mind? — Don't eat.

Can you feel with your heart? — Don't eat.

Will you obey with your will ? — Don't eat.

Adam and Eve chose to eat and, as the federal head and therefore official representative of humanity, they brought sin into the world. And, with sin came its inseparable companions of decay, weed, pollution, disease, cancer, corruption and death.

Every crushed heart, every broken body, every disturbed mind — the collective tears of the human race can trace their roots back to the sin of Adam and Eve in the Garden of Eden. And, with that sin a chasm separated a God whose holiness is as a consuming fire and a people who, born with a sinful nature, commit sinful acts. If left to his just deserts, the epitaph over mankind could be written in a few words:

World, here lies the man

Created to reign.

He disobeyed God,

Life was all in vain.

But, God did not leave man to his just deserts. Instead, the all-powerful Creator revealed His eternal plan of redemption, a plan so simple that the most unlearned can comprehend it — so profound that the most educated cannot exhaust it — so loving that eternity itself will not be sufficient to proclaim it — so powerful that no force in heaven or earth could withstand it — and so

mysterious that it would take a Lamb that will one day
roar like a Lion to unfold it. Man's extremity became
God's opportunity.

Sin had entered front and center onto the stage of human history. Man's image in the likeness of his Creator was marred, his fellowship with God broken, his right to rule as king of the earth forfeited — he was about to be expelled from the Garden of Eden to start his long, lonely, futile walk across the centuries. It was mankind's darkest hour.

2

A Word of Hope

For many people, 'hope' is simply the balancing of probabilities. A man wants to play golf. He looks out the window and says, "I 'hope' it doesn't rain today" — but he knows it might. A college coed shares a concern with her roommate: "I 'hope' I passed the exam" — but she knows she may have failed it. Sometimes 'hope' is used as a synonym for despair. After visiting a terminally ill patient, a loved one remarks, "All he has left is 'hope'." That is, everything has been done which can be done, and only a miracle can alter the inevitable march toward death.

In marked contrast, when the Creator of all things extends to mankind a word of 'hope', it is certain, absolute, unalterable, because God's word of promise is rooted in His unchanging character and infinite arm of power.

Sin had entered front and center onto the stage of human history. Man's image in the likeness of his Creator was marred, his fellowship with God broken, his right to rule as king of the earth forfeited — he was about to be expelled from the Garden of Eden to start his long, lonely, futile walk across the centuries. It was mankind's darkest hour. And, in the darkness of that hour, an eternal God who changes not gave to man a word of 'hope'.

Like a flaming meteor, it lit up the darkness of night to point to a glorious day. The 'hope' was couched in the promise that a personality would one day appear. His coming would have three objectives: first, to make it possible for man to be restored to the image of God with a mind with which he could think God's thoughts, with a heart with which he could respond to God's love, and with a will with which he could do God's bidding; second, to recapture man's lost destiny as king of the earth; and third, to defeat Satan, the fallen angelic being who, through the serpent, beguiled Adam and Eve in the Garden of Eden.

This promised Redeemer would be neither cherub nor seraph — a being from the angelic sphere would not do. God's word of 'hope' specifically referred to the Seed of a woman (Gen. 3:15). It was a man who caused man's dilemma — it would be a Man who would resolve it — the God-Man.

The God of creation, the God of eternity, the God who is all-knowing and all-powerful, was confident that the promised Seed could not be deterred from the divinely appointed task. And so, in the active will of God, a man was summoned from Ur of the Chaldees in the Mesopotamian Valley. The 'state' religion of Ur was idolatry, but for some reason this man believed in the one true God. Abram, whose name would later be changed to Abraham, would become the first "Hebrew", coming from a root word probably meaning "to cross over". In obedience to God, Abraham left his homeland and "crossed over" the Euphrates River on his way to the land of promise.

Through the loins of this man, God would start a new nation. And for that nation God would provide a land. And through that nation, in that land, God would provide the Seed — the Seed promised in Genesis 3:15 —

the Seed which could meet every need of the human heart for time and eternity. And since that Seed would one day deal Satan a fatal head wound, the destruction of the "chosen" people to prevent that Seed from being born would be one of Satan's most vigorous undertakings. It is for that reason that God said to Abraham and his seed, *"And I will bless them that bless thee, and curse him that curseth thee . . ."* (Gen. 12:3). The welfare of humanity is inseparably woven in the fabric of the spiritual and physical well-being of the Jewish people.

But, God did not choose the Jewish people because they were a large nation. He said through Moses, *"The Lord did not set his love upon you, nor choose you, because ye were more in number than any people; for ye were the fewest of all people"* (Dt. 7:7). Nor did He choose them because they were righteous, for He said, *"Understand, therefore, that the Lord thy God giveth thee not this good land to possess for thy righteousness; for thou art a stiff-necked people"* (Dt. 9:6). God is sovereign in His universe. He doesn't come down in the still of the night and call for a committee meeting — He doesn't ask for national elections — He doesn't ask man's permission to execute His plan. God does things according to His own good pleasure, and unless man realizes that God is sovereign in His universe, he will always build his castles on a foundation of sand, certain to one day collapse.

God chose Israel because He chose them! But once He did, they became *"the apple of his eye"* (Zech. 2:8), and woe unto angels, nations or individuals who, knowingly or unknowingly, seek to frustrate the divine design for human redemption. The continuous, relentless persecution of the Jewish people has not been the result of abrasive character, or disproportionate wealth, or great influence, but a Satanic attempt to defeat God and His plan of redemption for fallen humanity. Make no mistake about it, he will fail!

The universe didn't just happen. God created it. He threw the stars into space, He spoke the earth into existence, He fashioned Adam from the dust of the earth and breathed into him the breath of life, and from Adam's rib God formed woman. It ought not, therefore, seem impossible or be thought unreasonable that when Abraham was one hundred years old and Sarah ninety, a miraculous child should be born to this godly couple. The child was Isaac, the second son of Abraham. And the Lord made it clear that Isaac, the second-born, would have the right of heirship — God said, "... *in Isaac shall thy seed be called"* (Gen. 21:12).

In manhood, Isaac and his beautiful wife, Rebekah, were the proud parents of twin sons. Perhaps never were twins more dissimilar. Dissimilar in appearance — the elder son was ruddy and hairy, the younger son was not. Dissimilar in life styles — the elder son was a great hunter and a man of the field, the younger son was a plain man dwelling in tents. Dissimilar in that the elder son lived for the passing moment, the younger son for the promise of the future. Dissimilar in that the elder son was the object of Isaac's affection, the younger son of Rebekah's love. Dissimilar in that their stations in life were reversed — Esau was the older, the heir apparent, the one through whom the "promised seed" should have come; but God, who is too loving to be unkind and too wise to make a mistake, declared, "... *the elder shall serve the younger"* (Gen. 25:23). Jacob, therefore, would be in the lineage through which the promised Seed would come.

With the passing of time, Jacob had twelve sons, and the twelve sons became the respective heads of the twelve tribes of Israel which bore their names. How would the promised Seed be recognized when He appeared? For what good would it be to have the promise of a Redeemer but not be able to identify Him when He came into the world? God continued, therefore, to blaze a trail that men of faith would be able to follow. On his deathbed, Jacob summoned his twelve sons and gave them his 'last will and testament', forecasting that which would befall each of the twelve tribes of Israel. To his fourth-born son he said, *"The scepter shall not depart from Judah. . ."* (Gen. 49:10). The scepter was the emblem of the king, and Jacob was saying that the promised Seed would come through the tribe of Judah and not the other eleven tribes.

And so, men looked, waited, wondered and prayed for the One who alone could satisfy every requirement of mankind. Hundreds of years passed — it appeared as though God had forgotten His promise of a Redeemer or, worse, was powerless to bring His plan to fruition. But God was neither forgetful nor impotent.

With perfect precision and right on schedule, He reached down to a young lad who was the keeper of his father's sheep. This lad would become the first divinely appointed king of Israel. He was the tenth generation of the tribe of Judah — the tribe through which the promised Seed would come. His name was David, and it would be under David and his son, Solomon, that Israel would reach its zenith of power and glory — a glory unequaled in the last three thousand years. To David, God made a remarkable promise:

> *And when thy days be fulfilled, and thou shalt sleep with thy fathers, I will set up thy seed after thee, which shall proceed out of thine own body, and I will establish his kingdom . . . And thine house and thy kingdom shall be established forever before thee; thy*

throne shall be established forever.
                    2 Samuel 7:12, 16

King David was so overwhelmed by the divine promise that, in characteristic humility, he responded:

. . . Who am I, O Lord God? And what is my house, that thou hast brought me thus far? . . . Wherefore, thou art great, O Lord God; for there is none like thee, neither is there any God beside thee, according to all that we have heard with our ears . . . And now, O Lord God, the word that thou hast spoken concerning thy servant, and concerning his house, establish it forever, and do as thou hast said.
                    2 Samuel 7:18, 22, 25

King David rightly understood that the Seed of the woman, promised in Genesis 3:15, the Seed that would meet every need of the human race, the Seed that would come through his father Abraham, through Isaac not Ishmael, through Jacob not Esau, through Judah not the other eleven tribes, was to come into the world through his family — what a glorious privilege was his!

Once more, long, seemingly endless centuries passed with sufferings and groanings, with dispersion and restoration of the chosen race. And somehow, miraculously, they were neither annihilated nor assimilated. Marching armies couldn't stamp them out and surrounding nations couldn't integrate them. They were, as God had decreed, the indestructible Jew (Jer. 31:31-40). Then, when everything was ready — in *"the fullness of time"*, at God's precise moment — He sent His Son into the world. Miraculously born of the virgin Mary and, therefore, without the Adamic sin nature which was passed on to all of mankind, the Seed of the woman was now physically present among humanity. The endless dreams and hopes and needs of suffering humanity could now find solution in Him. Clearly, it was the noon hour of the human race. The eternal God was now present among His creation. Now Satan could be defeated, fellowship between God and man restored, and His glorious kingdom established.

This unparalleled event is recorded in the first verse of the first chapter of the first book of the New Testament. It simply and sublimely states, *"The book of the genealogy of Jesus Christ, the son of David, the son of Abraham."* And with that advent, the outlook for man never loomed brighter than it did at that moment. The hope of the ages was now present with the virgin birth of an infant Babe, dressed in swaddling clothes, born in a stable in the "little town of Bethlehem".

To suggest that mere men maneuvered and manipulated to make the myriad of events surrounding the birth of Christ fit the Old Testament pattern is ludicrous. Far easier would it be to disassemble a complex watch, throw the dismembered parts into a running clothes dryer and believe that in due course, given enough time, the watch would be whole, running and on time — to the very second.

3

The Incarnation

During the course of human history, there have been many great men. A few, like Washington and Lincoln, have their birthdays remembered because those days have become national holidays. None, however, have both their birth and death commemorated — none, that is, except for Jesus Christ. At Christmas, millions of people the world over remember His birth. At Easter, the same multitudes reflect on His death. All men are born to live, Jesus was born to die. It is His unique birth which gives inexhaustible meaning and infinite worth to His death.

Each Christmas, men look back more than nineteen hundred years to the birth of the Son of God. But, for more than four thousand years, men living on the other side of the incarnation eagerly looked forward to that same event.

The birth of God's Son was no accident; it was not the result of unforeseen or uncontrollable events. The all-knowing Creator and Sustainer of all things is never caught off guard. God does not respond to human events; He superintends them. Nowhere is this divine omniscience more clearly seen or more profoundly delineated than in the birth of the Lord Jesus Christ.

The eternal God, through the prophets of Israel, gave clear, detailed prophecies concerning the promised Seed who was one day to step onto the stage of human history. It has been stated that the Messiah had to come through the seed of Abraham, through the tribe of Judah and through the family of David. But additionally, He had to have a legal right to the throne of David (Isa. 9:7), be born of a virgin (Isa. 7:14), in Bethlehem (Mic. 5:2), and be God (Isa. 9:6). These identification characteristics were clear, inviolable and penned more than five hundred years before Christ was born.

The Old Testament is replete with Satanically-inspired attempts to destroy the blood line of the promised Messiah. Among them, the intermarriage of the sons of God and the daughters of men (Gen. 6:2) was an attempt to corrupt the human race and prevent the coming of the Seed. The decree of Pharaoh to kill all the newborn male children among the Jews (Ex. 1:22), the attempt of Athaliah to exterminate the royal seed (2 Ki. 11:1), and the Egyptian, Assyrian and Babylonian captivities with the attendant dangers of assimilation of the Jewish people, were all attempts to keep the promised Seed from His appointed task.

Many times it appeared that the coming of a Messiah who could meet the required conditions had been rendered impossible.

With infinite power, however, God overruled man's wickedness and actually made it serve His plan for human redemption. To King David, God made two unchangeable and irrevocable promises (Ps. 89:4). First, He promised that the throne of David would be everlasting and, second, that his physical seed would sit upon his throne (2 Sam. 7:16). David was unconditionally promised that lineal descendants of his would be preserved to sit upon that throne. Ultimately, these promises would find fulfillment in the Person of the Messiah — David's greater Son.

The Bible declares that David had several sons; however, the legal right to sit upon the throne passed to only one of them, King Solomon (1 Ki. 1:30). Only those who were of the kingly line inherited throne rights. Put another way, it was possible to be a physical descendant of David and yet have no legal right to sit upon the throne of Israel.

The first chapter of the Gospel of Matthew, written principally to the first-century Jew, lists the descendants of David who were in the royal lineage. This genealogy terminates with Joseph, the betrothed husband of Mary (Mt. 1:16). The fourteenth descendant of David in the royal lineage was a king called Jeconiah (Coniah). However, because of sin, God pronounced a curse on Jeconiah:

> *Thus saith the Lord, Write this man childless, a man that shall not prosper in his days; for no man of his seed shall prosper, sitting upon the throne of David, and ruling any more in Judah.*
>
> *Jeremiah 22:30*

This curse placed on Jeconiah by God did not say that he would never have any children, but that none of his descendants could occupy the throne of David.

Here, then, was an apparently insoluble problem — those who had the legal rights to the throne were barred from occupying it by the curse of Jeconiah.

Joseph, the espoused husband of Mary, was a direct descendant of Jeconiah. This means that, although Joseph inherited the legal right to the throne of David because he was of the kingly line of Solomon, he could not sit upon the throne because he came under the curse placed on the descendants of Jeconiah. The implication is clear, critical and irrefutable — if Jesus had been the physical son of Joseph, He too would come under the curse pronounced on Jeconiah's seed and would not be able to sit upon the throne of David and rule over Israel.

This posed a humanly impossible dilemma. Three main conditions had to be met to substantiate authenticity of the Messiah. These conditions appeared impossible to fulfill:

1. Jesus had to be a LINEAL descendant of David (in order to fulfill God's promise to David — that his seed would sit upon his throne).

2. He also had to be the LEGAL son of Joseph in order to inherit the right to sit upon the throne of David.

3. And yet, He could not be the PHYSICAL son of Joseph without coming under God's curse on Jeconiah.

Had the inspired penmen written themselves into an untenable corner with no possible escape? And since they claimed divine inspiration, was God himself in error and impotent? Could such an apparent dilemma ever be resolved? Indeed it could — but only by an infinite God who solved the problem by the miracle of the virgin birth. In Matthew, chapter one, the genealogy of David is traced to Joseph. Jesus, however, was not the physical son of Joseph. This can be stated with certainty because, at the time of the birth of Jesus, Joseph had never known Mary as his wife (Mt. 1:25). Jesus was, however, the legal son of Joseph (through adoption) and thereby inherited the right to the throne of David. Jesus was the legal son of Joseph, even though He was not his physical son. One condition, however, still posed a problem. The prophets of Israel prophesied that the Messiah would be a lineal descendant of David. Was this condition met?

The answer is found in the Gospel of Luke, where the

family tree of Mary, the mother of Jesus, is recorded. Mary was a direct descendant of David, not through King Solomon, upon whom the curse of Jeconiah fell, but through another son of David named Nathan (Lk. 3:23-31). Therefore, the curse on Jeconiah did not affect Mary or her actual son.

To summarize then: Jesus was the LINEAL son of Mary and, therefore, a direct descendant of David. In Jesus, God's promise to David (that he would always have a son to sit upon his throne) is fulfilled. Jesus was the LEGAL son of Joseph (by adoption) and thereby inherited the legal right to sit on the throne of David. But, He was not the PHYSICAL son of Joseph and thereby escaped the curse on Jeconiah.

Now, the question must be asked: "Who worked out this amazing and wonderful mosaic of circumstances?" To suggest that mere man maneuvered and manipulated to make the myriad of events surrounding the birth of Christ fit the Old Testament pattern is ludicrous. Far easier would it be to disassemble a complex watch, throw the dismembered parts into a running clothes dryer and believe that in due course, given enough time, the watch would be whole, running and on time – to the very second.

Design requires a designer. In the case of the birth of the Lord Jesus Christ, the eternal God moved the events of the centuries to bring His Son onto the stage of human history exactly as He had promised. There is no intellectually honest alternative and no greater evidence of the faithfulness of God to His Word, which has been forever settled in the heavens (Ps. 119:89).

The atmosphere created by the peace,
— the travel permitted by the roads,
— the communication enabled by a common language and philosophy,
— and the restlessness engendered by a religious vacuum,
all consorted to make that precise moment "the fullness of time" — everything was ready at the moment when the Son of God chose to pay an "in-flesh" visit to the people of the planet Earth.

4

In the Fullness of Time

A gifted friend framed a haunting melody with these beautiful words:

> *Love was when God became a man,*
> *Locked in time and space, without rank or place.*
> *Love was God, born of Jewish kin,*
> *Just a carpenter with some fishermen.*
> *Love was when Jesus walked in history,*
> *Lovingly He brought a new life that's free . . . .*

It was love that prompted God to become a man, to walk in history. But, this was no idle whim or last-minute effort to salvage a lost creation. The only alternative to planning is to respond to circumstances — but, the eternal God does not shoot from the hip. He does not respond to history, He originates and superintends it through His direct or permissive will. Because He is the Alpha and Omega, the First and the Last, the One who alone knows all things, the perpetual contemporary, His timing is always perfect. He is never caught off guard or unprepared.

And so it was, in *"the fullness of time"* (Gal. 4:4), that God sent His Son into the world. At least two thousand years earlier, the promise of that Seed was given. Everything in the Old Testament Scriptures was moving toward that moment.

His time of coming was prophesied:

> *Know, therefore, and understand, that from the going forth of the commandment to restore and to build Jerusalem* [445 B.C.] *unto the Messiah, the Prince, shall be seven weeks, and threescore and two weeks* [483 years] *;the street shall be built again, and the wall, even in troublous times. And after threescore and two weeks shall Messiah be cut off* [April 32 A.D.]
> *Daniel 9:25-26a*

His place of coming was proclaimed:

> *But thou, Bethlehem Ephrathah, though thou be little among the thousands of Judah, yet out of thee shall he come forth unto me that is to be ruler in Israel, whose goings forth have been from of old, from everlasting.*
> *Micah 5:2*

His way of coming was described:

> *Therefore the Lord himself shall give you a sign; Behold, the virgin shall conceive, and bear a son, and shall call his name Immanuel.*
> *Isaiah 7:14*

His purpose for coming was revealed:

> *. . . It is a light thing that thou shouldest be my servant to raise up the tribes of Jacob, and to restore the preserved of Israel; I will also give thee for a light to the nations, that thou mayest be my salvation unto the end of the*

earth.

Isaiah 49:6

His position at His coming was designated:

> *For unto us a child is born, unto us a son is given, and the government shall be upon his shoulder; and his name shall be called Wonderful, Counselor, The Mighty God, The Everlasting Father, The Prince of Peace.*
>
> *Isaiah 9:6*

In the seven yearly appointments or holidays which God gave to Israel (Lev. 23), the Messiah's redemptive ministry was chronologized, from His death (Passover) until His second coming to dwell among men (Tabernacles). And, in the priesthood and sacrificial system, His work was typified and illustrated.

Not without reason, therefore, the collective hopes and dreams of the ages met in that stable in the little village of Bethlehem, in the Judean hills, in the obscure land of Israel. It was the noon hour of human history — it was *"the fullness of time"*. The infinite, eternal Creator was now walking among His creation.

It was *"the fullness of time"* because of world peace. For the first time in centuries, the civilized world knew a repose from fighting and killing. The Roman army was cruel and ruthless, but its power was so great, its appearance so formidable that no nation would dare challenge her 'universal' rule. At the apex of Rome's might and power, a lowly Babe was born who would one day rule the ages with a peace predicated on love not hate, on justice not inequity, on righteousness not force.

It was *"the fullness of time"* because of Roman roads. To keep peace in the world she had captured, Rome sent her legions to her far-flung empire. And wherever her soldiers marched, her engineers built highways. "All roads lead to Rome" was not an empty cliche' or a meaningless hyperbole – they did! Travelers to Europe and the Middle East can still see vestiges of those same roads and Roman engineering skill. But, roads from Rome to her vast empire could be traveled in both directions. The ambassadors of the Son of God could use those same highways to herald the message of the King. This is one of the reasons for rapid spread and growth of Christianity in the centuries immediately following Christ's death, burial, resurrection and ascension.

It was *"the fullness of time"* because of Greek culture. Before the emergence of Rome, between the years 356 B.C. and 323 B.C., Alexander the Great conquered much of the known world. And wherever his soldiers went in military conquest, his philosophers, educators and artisans were soon to be found. He propagated the Greek language and culture. A 'one-language' world with a 'one-philosophy' world view would be much easier to penetrate with the glorious Gospel. There was no need to spend two years in language study. Courses in culture were unnecessary. Travel was much safer and the stranger was subject to less hostility.

It was *"the fullness of time"* because of great religious expectation. Of the worshiping of gods, of mystery religions, of spiritual activity there was no limit. But, man-made religion can never satisfy – it can never quench the thirsting of the soul. Historians and theologians inform us that the religious anticipation of the first century was acute and widespread. There was a spiritual void. Into that vacuum the Son of God came.

The atmosphere created by the peace,
   – the travel permitted by the roads,
   – the communication enabled by a common language and philosophy,

    — and the restlessness engendered by a religious
      vacuum,

all consorted to make that precise moment *"the fullness of time"* — everything was ready at the moment when the Son of God chose to pay an "in-flesh" visit to the people of the planet Earth. The *"day star"* had now appeared with *"healing in his wings"*.

The one requisite for establishing His earthly kingdom was that Israel turn from her sin. At the Temple, the pulsebeat and heartbeat of the nation could be felt as nowhere else. Had they met the one requisite? Had they repented?

5

Unto His Own

The Lord Jesus Christ is the Son of God (Mt. 3:16-17). He is also the son of David (Mt. 1:1). The Prophet Isaiah captured this dichotomy in his inspired and oft-quoted words, *"For unto us a CHILD is born, unto us a SON is given . . . "* (Isa. 9:6). In time, on the planet Earth, in the insignificant land of Israel, in the obscure village of Bethlehem, a CHILD was born. But, that Child was also the preexistent SON of God (Mic. 5:2). The beloved physician Luke made this same observation when he recorded the angelic message to Mary, *"He shall be great, and shall be called the SON of the Highest; and the Lord God shall give unto him the throne of his FATHER, DAVID"* (Lk. 1:32). From a DIVINE standpoint, He would be *"The Son of the Highest";* from a HUMAN standpoint, He would be given *"the throne of his father, David."* Jesus Christ, as the son of David (both His real mother, Mary, and His legal father, Joseph, were of the lineage of David, Mt. 1; Lk. 3), was rightful heir to the throne of Israel.

At His birth, wise men came from the East inquiring, *"Where is he that is born King of the Jews?"* (Mt. 2:2); and at His death, the Roman ruler Herod had these words placed on His cross, *"THIS IS JESUS, THE KING OF THE JEWS"* (Mt. 27:37).

It was customary in biblical times for kings to send out a herald or forerunner. The forerunner's job was to go before his king and announce to the people that the king was coming. The multitudes were then, as it were, to sweep the sidewalk, whitewash the fence, bring in the children's bicycles, straighten up the porch — in general, clean the area through which the king would be coming, for this was the king's highway. During a recent visit of an American president to Russia and China those nations spent millions of dollars beautifying the highway between the airport and the place where the president would be staying. Truly, there is little new under the sun.

It was the privilege of John the Baptist to be the herald of the Lord Jesus Christ — his responsibility was to announce the King's coming. His ministry fulfilled the words of the Prophet Isaiah:

> *The voice of him that crieth in the wilderness, Prepare ye the way of the Lord, make straight in the desert a highway for our God. Every valley shall be exalted, and every mountain and hill shall be made low; and the crooked shall be made straight, and the rough places plain.*
>
> *Isaiah 40:3-4*

As the herald of the King, John the Baptist pled with Israel to *"Repent; for the kingdom of heaven is at hand"* (Mt. 3:2). He was not, however, speaking of external cleansing, but internal cleansing. The One whose coming he heralded was both human and divine, and the kingdom which John spoke of was at hand in that, if the nation repented of its sin, Jesus as the son of David and heir to the throne of Israel would establish a literal kingdom on the earth. The form of government by which Jesus would govern was presented in His sermon on the mount. First, He identified the character of those who would become citizens of the kingdom (Mt. 5:1-16); second, He established the principles of righteousness in the kingdom (Mt. 5:17-7:12); and finally, He invited men to the kingdom (Mt. 7:13-27).

Following John's beheading by Herod, which was the beginning of the handwriting on the wall (that repentance, the one requisite for establishing the kingdom, would not be met), Jesus continued proclaiming the same message as that of His forerunner, *"Repent; for the kingdom of heaven is at hand"* (Mt. 4:17). And, still later, He commanded His disciples to share the very same message of hope, *"Go not into the way of the Gentiles . . . But go, rather, to the lost sheep of the house of Israel. And as ye go, preach, saying, The kingdom of heaven is at hand"* (Mt. 10:5-7). Since Jesus was the rightful heir to the throne of David, it was to the Jewish people exclusively that Jesus was offering Himself as King. For this reason, He told His disciples to *"Go not into the way of the Gentiles . . ."* (Mt. 10:5). Did Jesus not die for all mankind? Was He not the Savior of the Gentile as well as the Jew? Why then this prohibition? A statesman running for the office of President of the United States of America cannot be elected by Canadian and Mexican votes. It is American citizens who can, by their votes, place him into office. Jesus had the proper credentials to rule over Israel. But, they would have to demonstrate their desire to have Him rule by turning to God from their sin.

The conflict and skirmishes between Jesus and the Jewish leadership could go on no longer. A clash was imminent.

On Palm Sunday, one week before the Jewish feast of Passover, Jesus descended the Mount of Olives, passed through the Kidron Valley, climbed the hill on the other side, entered Jerusalem through the Eastern Gate and made His way to the Temple. The one requisite for establishing His earthly kingdom was that Israel repent. At the Temple, the pulsebeat and heartbeat of the nation could be felt as nowhere else. Had they met the one requisite? Had they repented?

At the Temple He found sellers of animals and changers of money. Passover was one of the three yearly Jewish festivals (Pentecost and Tabernacles were the other two) when the people were commanded by the Mosaic law to worship at the Temple in Jerusalem (Dt. 16:16). Many, living out of the land, had to make long, difficult and often dangerous journeys to reach the Temple. Carrying a sacrificial lamb hundreds of miles for Passover was impossible — a lamb would have to be purchased — and foreign currency had to be exchanged if the visiting worshiper was to be able to go about his business. At the Temple the cost of purchasing an "acceptable" Passover lamb (one without spot or blemish and with priestly approval) was excessively high and the exchange rate in currency became a money-making scheme for the Temple leaders. Here, then, were devout Jews who had made the trek to Jerusalem to worship the God of Israel, and they were being "ripped off" by their own religious leaders.

When Jesus saw the corruption, in righteous indignation He turned over the tables of the "merchandisers", drove them out of the Temple and said, *"It is written, My house shall be called the house of prayer, but ye have made it a den of thieves"* (Mt. 21:13). It was now that elements from within the national leadership (not the common people) began to seek His life. Jesus of Nazareth had become a threat to their corrupt practices and distorted theology.

The one requirement for His setting up of a kingdom was repentance — that one requisite was not forthcoming. From a human perspective, the Jewish leadership was responsible for the rejection of their Messiah. From a divine perspective, to this end God had appointed them (Rom. 11:8-11). Now the good news of salvation through Christ's death and resurrection would go to both Gentile and Jew, and the promise made to Abraham that *". . . in thy seed shall all the nations of the earth be blessed. . ."* (Gen. 22:18) would find fulfillment.

Jesus went out of the city and, from the depths of His loving and compassionate heart, He wept. Soon He would say, *"If thou hadst known, even thou, at least in this thy day, the things which belong unto thy peace! But now they are hidden from thine eyes"* (Lk. 19:42). And again, *"O Jerusalem, Jerusalem, thou that killest the prophets, and stonest them who are sent unto thee, how often would I have gathered thy children together, even as a hen gathereth her chickens under her wings, and ye would not* [have me] *!"* (Mt. 23:37).

A poet captured something of the pathos and tragedy of Israel's rejection of her greatest Son with these words:

Jerusalem, Jerusalem, enthroned once on high,
Thou favorite home of God on earth,
Thou heaven beneath the sky,
Now brought to bondage with thy sons,
A curse and grief to see,
Jerusalem, Jerusalem, our tears shall flow for thee.

O, hadst thou known thy day of grace,
And flocked beneath the wing
Of Him who called thee tenderly,
Thy own anointed King,
Then had the tribes of all the earth
Gone up, thy pomp to see,
And glory dwelt within thy gates and all thy sons
been free.

Jerusalem, Jerusalem, until thou turn again,
And seek with penitence of heart,
The Lamb thy sons have slain,

> *Till to the Savior of all mankind,*
> *Thou humbly bow the knee,*
> *Jerusalem, Jerusalem, our tears shall flow for thee.*

But, did Israel stumble that they should fall? Is God vindictive? Was it the divine intent to simply punish Israel? Hear the answer from one of Israel's greatest sons and history's towering personalities. The Apostle Paul wrote, *". . . God forbid* [a strong idiom meaning don't even think such a thought]; *but rather through their fall salvation is come unto the Gentiles"* (Rom. 11:11). In the very stumbling of Israel, God's redemptive plan for all of mankind would be implemented (Rom. 11:12). Concerning thus truth, the inspired penman could only write:

> *Oh, the depth of the riches both of the wisdom and knowledge of God! How unsearchable are his judgments, and his ways past finding out!*
>
> *Romans 11:33*

"But, His cup was not yet full. As Christ hung on the cross between Heaven and earth, He had to drink to the bitter dregs the agony of 'forsakenness'. For there on that cruel tree, Jesus was forsaken by His eternal Father."

6

Forsaken

Loneliness is a tragic thing to experience. Ask the woman who does her shopping at four food stores, buying a few items at each stop so she can chat for a moment with the clerk. Ask the old man whose wife is deceased and children live in faraway places, as he stares listlessly out the window. Ask the teenager whose parents are too busy to give time or show affection.

But, if loneliness is tragic, to be "forsaken" is far worse. Forsaken means "to leave", "to utterly abandon". Jesus was forsaken to a degree that no other man has ever known — He was forsaken utterly and utterly forsaken.

Jesus was forsaken by the world He created. John wrote, *"All things were made by him; and without him was not anything made that was made"* (Jn. 1:3). The Bible opens with the statement, *"In the beginning God created the heaven and the earth"* (Gen. 1:1). He came to the world He fashioned by the word of His power, but the world said , "No thank you, we're not interested." The world would not receive Him (Jn. 1:10).

Jesus was forsaken by the nation from which He sprang. He was from the seed of Abraham, the tribe of Judah, the family of David. He was a Jew according to the flesh. If any nation should have been open and responsive to His message and Person, it should have been Israel, But, *"He came unto his own /creation/, and his own [nation] received him not"* (Jn. 1:11).

Jesus was forsaken by the village He lived in. He was called a Nazarene because He lived in the village of Nazareth nestled in the beautiful Galilean hills fifteen miles west of the Sea of Galilee. Here he spent His childhood days running and playing and growing into manhood. Here He doubtless helped His father in the carpentry shop. But in Nazareth, in adulthood, He could do no mighty miracles because they did not believe in Him (Lk. 4:23-24). And concerning Nazareth, Jesus would say, *". . . A prophet is not without honor, except in his own country. . ."* (Mt. 13:57), or put positively, *". . . A prophet has honor except in his own country. . ."* In Nazareth He preached His first sermon (Lk. 4:16-24) and left never to return. And so, He was forsaken by the village He lived in. Here is an amazing example that all too often "familiarity breeds contempt".

Jesus was forsaken by the brothers He grew up with. Mary and Joseph had other children — they were half brothers to Jesus (Mt. 13:55-56). Having been raised in the same house, seeing Him up close, knowing the reality of the Holy Spirit's comment, *"And Jesus increased in wisdom and stature, and in favor with God and man"* (Lk. 2:52), it would be reasonable to assume that they would have embraced Him. But, the Word of God declares that they did not believe in Him until after His death, burial and resurrection (Jn. 7:5). Amazingly, He was forsaken by the brothers He grew up with.

Jesus was forsaken by the disciples He trained. For three years they ate with Him, slept with Him, were taught by Him. They saw Him feed the hungry, heal the lame, raise the dead and control the elements. When He declared that all would forsake Him, Peter, with a sincere but all-too-human bravado, proclaimed, *"Though all men shall be offended because of thee, yet will I never be offended"* (Mt. 26:33). A few hours later and less than a mile away, Peter would respond to an inquiry concerning his association with Jesus by saying, *". . . I know him not"* (Lk. 22:57). Nor was the big fisherman alone. Long centuries before, the inspired penman wrote, *". . .smite the shepherd, and the sheep shall be scattered . . ."* (Zech. 13:7). And with His death, the disciples fled in fear and defeat — their world had come unglued. He was forsaken by His disciples.

But, His cup was not yet full. As Christ hung on the cross between Heaven and earth, He had to drink to the bitter dregs the agony of "forsakenness". For there on that cruel tree, Jesus was forsaken by His eternal Father. And, in the anguish of that moment, the Son of God cried out, *"My God, my God, why has thou forsaken me?"* (Mt. 27:46). The agony, the emotion, the pathos of that event can never be fully comprehended by mortal man. In that instant the sins of the world were placed on the spotless Lamb. He who knew no sin was made sin for us that we might be made the righteousness of God in Him (2 Cor. 5:21). And, a holy God who is a consuming fire could not look upon His Son who bore our sins in His own body on the tree (1 Pet. 2:24).

The Sovereign of the universe, the One who created all things by the word of His power and through whom all things adhere, walked on the planet Earth and among its people for thirty-three years. He was forsaken by the world He created, the nation He sprang from, the village He lived in, the brothers He grew up with, the disciples He trained, and the Father He had eternally fellowshipped with.

Jesus was forsaken that you and I, through faith in Him, need never be. Here then, is grace — grace greater than all our sin.

"He had not yet been betrayed . . . but He knew He was soon to die. He knew the precise moment, the exact location and by whose hand."

7

This is the Day Which the Lord Hath Made

Did you ever think that the death of Christ on Calvary was a crushing defeat? Did you perhaps think that the situation had gotten out of control? Did you think that God was caught off guard? Did you think that the crucifixion of the Son of Man was unplanned or unanticipated? If you did, then think again!

A few short hours before the Lord's crucifixion, He commanded His disciples to make ready the Passover (Mt. 26:18). He expressed His feelings this way: *". . . With desire I have desired to eat this passover with you before I suffer"* (Lk. 22:15). The main element of the Passover was the lamb. It was slain, it suffered – but through that suffering it brought redemption to multitudes of Jews enslaved in Egypt. Jesus knew that He would soon suffer and die as the Passover Lamb. He knew that through that death He would bring redemption to countless multitudes who, through the ages, would put their trust in Him. But first, He wanted to eat the Passover lamb before He became the Passover Lamb. It would be a source of encouragement – a vivid reminder that His death would not be in vain. He had not yet been betrayed – He had not yet been taken captive

— He had not yet been tried — but He knew He was soon to die. He knew the precise moment, the exact location and by whose hand.

And so, in obedience, the disciples made ready the Passover, and they ate together. Following the dinner, they sang an hymn and went out into the Mount of Olives (Mt. 26:30). Did you know that we, today, in the twentieth century, so long removed from that event, know the song that they sang? It has been sung by Jews down through the centuries in connection with the Passover. It is called the Great Hallel and is taken from Psalm 118. In the official book (Haggadah), detailing the observance of the Passover and produced under the supervision of the Chief Rabbi of Israel, two verses of Scripture from Psalm 118 must be recited twice during the Passover dinner. The first verse is, *"This is the day which the Lord hath made; we will rejoice and be glad in it"* (Ps. 118:24). Many people think that this is a verse for all seasons. There is the man who bounds out of bed on a glorious day, he feels good, the sun is shining, he has a pleasant schedule, and he gleefully proclaims, "This is the day which the Lord hath made; I will rejoice and be glad in it!" Then, there is the man who takes the other tack. He climbs out of bed, it's cold and dreary, his schedule is not a particularly pleasant one, but with bulldog determination and with stiff upper lip, he exclaims, "Well, in spite of it all, this is the day which the Lord hath made; I will rejoice and be glad in it."

Both miss the glorious point to be made. Jesus was not singing about any day or every day, He was speaking of a specific day, a definitive day — the day He would die on the cross of Calvary for the sins of the world. He fully understood the physical pain and spiritual agony to be endured — He realized that for the first time in all of eternity, the sins of the world would be placed upon Him, and He would be separated from His heavenly Father. But Jesus also knew that He was there by divine appointment. Had He not said, *"For even the Son of man came, not to be ministered unto but to minister, and to give his life a ransom for many"* (Mk. 10:45)? And, *"No man taketh it* [my life] *from me, but I lay it down of myself. I have power to lay it down, and I have power to take it again . . ."* (Jn. 10:18). And again concerning His death, He said, *". . . for this cause came I into the world. . ."* (Jn. 18:37). Since He was there in the plan and program of His Father, and since His death would provide redemption for those who put their trust in Him, He could sing in triumph, only hours before His death, *"This is the day which the Lord hath made; we will rejoice and be glad in it."* How utterly amazing!

And, as if that were not enough, He sang a second verse. And since He was both perfect Man and eternal God, His voice must have been beautiful with perfect pitch and resonance — nothing flat, nothing sharp and nothing discordant. And the lyrics — they were words of absolute victory for He sang, *"The stone which the builders refused is become the head of the corner"* (Ps. 118:22). The Stone was Christ. The builder was Israel. They had rejected His messianic claims, and now He would die. But, through that death, the true Church, including both Jew and Gentile, would spring forth into life. He, himself, would be its Cornerstone. A sovereign God was using Israel as His instrument for worldwide blessing — as He had promised — even during her period of sin and disobedience.

What, then, was the commentary of the Lord of glory only hours before His death which would turn the sky dark at midafternoon? Permit a solemn paraphrase: "I am here by the active design and power of My Father, and through My death I will become the Cornerstone upon which the true Church — My eternal bride — will be built." The psalmist could only comment, *"This is the Lord's doing; it is marvelous in our eyes"* (Ps. 118: 23).

With the death of Christ, the Jewish leaders thought they had finally gotten rid of a rabble-rouser; the disciples thought their hopes and dreams had come to an insoluble end; Satan thought he had finally destroyed the Seed who was to bruise his head and recapture man's lost destiny as king of the earth. Over His cross Rome wrote, "The King of the Jews". Satan thought that he had God's Son checkmated, a word coming from the Hebrew and meaning "The King is dead". But Satan's glee was premature and ill-advised. Only God knew the truth. His Son's physical death would consummate in His bodily resurrection — on the third day Christ rose from the grave. The King was very much alive.

Calvary was not an ignominious defeat but an indescribably glorious triumph — are you sharing in it?

Twentieth-century man, so far removed from that scene, can never fully comprehend the depths of despair to which the disciples had fallen at Christ's death, nor the heights of exaltation to which they were catapulted at His resurrection.

8

From the Depths of Despair to the Heights of Exaltation

With the death of Jesus, the hopes, dreams, longings and aspirations of the disciples came to a screeching halt. They had forsaken everything and followed Him for three years. They walked with Him, talked with Him, ate with Him, slept with Him, were taught by Him. They were convinced that He was going to lead them in revolt against the despised Romans. The Romans were oppressive. They ridiculed the religion of the Jews. They taxed them excessively. They ruled ruthlessly. Every red-blooded Israelite hated the Romans with a passion.

And Jesus, as the Son of David, was born King of the Jews — He had a legal right to rule over Israel. The Jewish Scriptures told of a Deliverer who would appear to break the yoke of Gentile oppression (Ezek. 34:27). It was not without reason, therefore, that the disciples viewed Jesus as their coming King. They inquired, *". . . Behold, we have forsaken all, and followed thee. What shall we have, therefore* [when you enter into Your kingdom]*?"* (Mt. 19:27). And the mother of James and John, zealous for her sons, requested, *". . . Grant that these, my two sons, may sit, the one on thy right hand, and the other on the left, in thy kingdom"* (Mt. 20:21).

And two blind beggars, hearing of Jesus' presence as He was leaving Jericho, cried out, *". . . Have mercy on us, O Lord, thou Son of David"* (Mt. 20:31) — King.

As "kingdom fever" was mounting on the part of the disciples, they climbed to the top of the Mount of Olives. It was approaching the 14th day of the Jewish month of Nisan and Passover. Perhaps as many as a million Jewish people had returned to Jerusalem from all over the known world to observe the Passover. Here, then, was the needed manpower to be lead in rebellion against despised Rome.

From the top of the Mount of Olives, Jesus and His disciples could look across the Kidron Valley to the glistening city of Jerusalem below. They could see the massive wall stretching around the city designed to keep out intruders. The sun was reflecting off of the beautiful stones and precious metals which adorned the Temple. The latter rains would have ended, and the pleasant April weather would have, by now, carpeted the rolling hills with green grass and multicolored wild flowers. The priests could be seen preparing for the onslaught of great crowds with their Passover lambs. The sights, the sounds, the smells all served to electrify that moment. And, in the midst of that atmosphere, Jesus turned to His disciples and said, "Go and get the donkey." These were Jewish disciples. They knew their Scriptures. They were familiar with the prophecy of Zechariah, *". . . behold, thy King cometh unto thee . . . lowly, and riding upon an ass, and upon a colt, the foal of an ass* (Zech. 9:9).

They placed Jesus upon that donkey, He started down the Mount of Olives, crossed through the narrow Kidron Valley, climbed the slope on the other side and entered the city through the Eastern Gate. Before Him stood the Temple in all of its splendor.

And during the processional, the multitude cut down palm branches, placed them before Him and cried out, ". . . *Hosanna to the Son of David! . . .*" (Mt. 21:9). Hosanna literally means "deliver now" or "save now". They were quoting directly from Psalm 118:25. They were not asking Him to save them from their sins. At that moment they had no concept of His death, burial and resurrection — that would come later. They were asking Him to deliver them from the oppressive heel of the hated Romans.

But everything appeared to be going astray, and the fickle multitudes who cried out "Hosanna" to the Son of David on one day would cry out "Crucify Him" the next day. Within hours, His life was torturously ebbing away as He hung between Heaven and earth on a Roman cross. The irony of that scene can never be fully comprehended or exhausted. Jesus was not dead because He fell off of a Judean hill. They weren't mourning because He was run over by a runaway chariot. He hadn't been set upon by thugs. No, He had been crucified on a Roman cross — by the very same people the disciples thought He was going to lead them in rebellion against. This One they thought was to be their King died like a common criminal at the hands of the enemies. How inglorious! And, with the death of Jesus, the disciples sank to the depths of defeat, despondency and despair. They were sure He it was who would lead them against Rome. But let them speak for themselves: *"But we hoped that it had been he who should have redeemed* [delivered] *Israel. . . "* (Lk. 24:21) — and now He's dead!

Low in the grave He lay — and the disciples thought that was the end, their hopes thrust through at the place called Calvary, their dreams unfulfilled, their longings unsatisfied. But on the third day — on the third day He rose from the grave and began to appear to His followers. He was alive — vitally, dynamically alive. Twentieth-century man, so far removed from that scene, can never fully comprehend the depths of despair to which the disciples had fallen at His death, nor the heights of exaltation to which they were catapulted at His resurrection.

He ministered to them for forty days and before leaving, He gave to those who belong to Him a final command: *"But ye shall receive power, after the Holy Spirit is come upon you; and ye shall be witnesses unto me both in Jerusalem, and in all Judea, and in Samaria, and unto the uttermost part of the earth"* (Acts 1:8). That command has never been annulled — it has never been rescinded — it has never been negated — it has never been abrogated. It comes down the corridor of time as authoritative today as it was the moment it was first given. His last command should be the Church's first concern. God had promised Abraham, two thousand years earlier, that in his seed all of the nations (Gentiles) would be blessed. Who, among the wisest sages of mankind, could ever have thought that through the chosen nation's rejection of her Messiah and His resultant death at Calvary and institution of the New Covenant the blessing of the glorious Gospel would flow freely to all peoples. We fall prostrate before the divine plan, remembering that our thoughts are not His thoughts, and our ways are not His ways (Isa. 55:8).

"As they were uprooted and driven from land to land, there was no haven at the end of the road, no protection along the way, and the everpresent danger of robbers and murderers."

9

How Dark the Night

Anti-Semitism is an ugly word. Just men have always abhorred it. But, like a bad dream, it refuses to go away. Historians, social scientists, philosophers, theologians — all are hard pressed to explain this perpetual phenomenon which is as ancient as Abraham, the father of the Jewish people, and as contemporary as the modern state of Israel.

In the Old Testament the Amorites, Egyptians, Amalekites, Assyrians, Phoenicians, Philistines, Babylonians, Persians and Macedonians were among the many nations who rose up to plunder and harass the sons of Jacob. In turn, each of these nations experienced the chastening hand of God and, with few exceptions, the nations of antiquity who persecuted the Jew are no more. That they existed at all is often only known through the Bible, a few ancient manuscripts or the archaeologist's spade.

Following the death of Christ, anti-Semitism not only continued but intensified.

Among her antagonists were Roman soldiers, Islamic fanatics, "Christian" Crusaders, Spanish Inquisitors, Russian Cossacks, Nazi S. S. troops and, most recently, Palestinian terrorists. No race, no religion, no nation, no ethnic group has experienced the continuous persecution that the descendants of Abraham, Isaac and Jacob have known. Clearly, one of the great marvels of human history is the continued existence of the Jewish race. God, himself, gave the formula for destroying His beloved nation. He said, in effect, that if a man could destroy the sun, moon and stars — then and only then could he destroy Israel. But as long as those heavenly bodies were in the sky, Israel would continue to exist as a nation (Jer. 31:31-40). Here is overwhelming evidence to an open mind of the existence of God and His faithfulness to His Word.

The universal dispersion of the Jewish people with its attendant persecution was prophesied by Moses almost fifteen hundred years before it came to pass:

> *And the Lord shall scatter thee among all people, from the one end of the earth even unto the other; and there thou shalt serve other gods, which neither thou nor thy fathers have known, even wood and stone. And among these nations shalt thou find no ease, neither shall the sole of thy foot have rest; but the Lord shall give thee there a trembling heart, and failing of eyes, and sorrow of mind. And thy life shall hang in doubt before thee; and thou shalt fear day and night, and shalt have no assurance of thy life.*
>
> *(Dt. 28:64-66)*

And Jesus, himself, in His message given on the Mount of Olives only a few short days before His crucifixion, said:

> *And when ye shall see Jerusalem compassed with armies, then know that its desolation is near . . . For there shall be great distress in*

*the land, and wrath upon this people. And
they shall fall by the edge of the sword, and
shall be led away captive into all nations; and
Jerusalem shall be trodden down by the Gentiles, until the times of the Gentiles be fulfilled.*

(Lk. 21:20, 23 - 24)

After the death of Christ the hostility between the
Jews and imperial Rome continued to fester for some
thirty years. Then the Roman governor, for some unknown reason, chose to loot the Temple and interfere
in Jewish worship. More than two hundred years earlier,
in 165 B.C., the Jews had successfully revolted against
the Greeks who had desecrated their Temple. Now they
would try to revolt against the Romans. For her part,
Rome sent a powerful army under the command of General Titus. The Jews took refuge behind the strong walls
of the city of Jerusalem, and the Romans countered by
building a barrier outside the city walls so that supplies
could not get in and people could not get out. Eventually, the starving defenders began to fight among themselves and finally, in 70 A.D., the city of Jerusalem fell.
The Temple was destroyed, precisely as the Lord Jesus
had predicted, and not one stone was left upon another
(Mt. 24:2). Thousands of Jews were crucified, and others
were sold as slaves or dragged off to be exhibited or
torn to pieces in Roman arenas. Those who could, fled
across the desert — some went east toward Babylon and
others southward toward Egypt and North Africa. Still
others chose to sail to the countries bordering the Mediterranean Sea. The worldwide dispersion of the Jews had
now begun.

Some Jews, however, stayed behind, preferring to bow
to imperial Rome than face the uncertainties and hard-
ships of dispersion. Sixty-five years later, in 135 A.D.,

these remaining Jews would seek to throw off the yoke of foreign oppression one more time. On this occasion, the esteemed Rabbi Akiba identified a leader by the name of Bar Kochba (Son of the Star) as the long-promised Messiah and Deliverer of Israel. With rabbinic sanction, multitudes flocked to his side to fight against Rome. It was a disaster. Half a million men, women and children died. Rabbi Akiba was captured and tortured to death, and now the Romans had had enough of the troublesome, freedom-loving Jews. The holy city of Jerusalem was leveled and plowed over. Jews were forbidden, by pain of death, to set foot in the new Roman city called Aelia Capitolina, which was built on the site. The name of the land was changed to Syria Philistina, from which would later come Palestine.

The Roman Empire, in the centuries which followed, began to decline and, in 476, fell by the weight of its own debauchery and corruption, and in the deserts of Arabia a new religion arose, with the flight of Mohammed from Mecca to Medina in 622 A.D. Familiar with both Judaism and Christianity, Mohammed took elements of both, added his own "revelation" and wrote the Koran, holy book of the Islamic faith. In the seventh century, his followers, with sword in hand, swept out of the Arabian desert and conquered lands from Persia to southern France. Israel was one of the many victims who fell within her domain. And in Jerusalem, on the site where Abraham had consented to offer Isaac as a sacrifice to his God and the Solomonic and Herodian Temples once stood, they erected the "Dome of the Rock" — today the third most holy site in the Moslem world. The Moslems held sway for the next five centuries. Under their rule the plight of the Jew was not good; but they fared better than they did under the Romans.

In the eleventh century, the "Christians" of Europe

became aroused over the reality that the holy land was ruled by the Moslems. Under Richard the Lion-Hearted, the Crusades were launched in 1095. The intent was to deliver the holy land from the infidel. As Crusader armies, seeking adventure, liquidation of debts and assurance of Heaven, marched across Europe, they killed, raped and robbed the Jews as they passed through their villages. The first contingent of Crusaders arrived in Israel in 1099. They rounded up the Jews, put them in the synagogue, locked the door, barred the gates and burned the men, women and children to death. Thus began the "Christian" cleansing of the land in which Jesus had died to bring peace to a sin-sick world.

The Crusaders managed to gain a foothold and for about one hundred years they controlled Israel from strategic fortresses along the coastline and inland. Eventually they were driven out by the savage troops from the eastern realm of Saladin. The holy land continued to be drenched in blood until it was captured by the Ottoman Turks in 1516. Under Turkish tutorage, the forests were cut down to fuel the locomotives, the hills became barren, the topsoil was washed away by the rains – the land was raped. The beautiful plains of Israel became swamps and swarms of mosquitoes spread malaria.

But that was not the end – more wars were to come. In 1798 Napoleon entered Israel from Egypt, hoping to destroy the Ottoman Empire. He was defeated at the coastal fortress of Acre, north of modern day Haifa, and returned to France.

And, the ancient land which knew greatness and glory in the days of David and Solomon, the land where Christ was born and the stage upon which redemption was acted out, lay in decay. It had become no more than a collection of sickly villages, with Jerusalem hardly more than a small town, and the whole country ruled by a governor appointed — usually for a price — by the sultan in Turkey.

Not in all of the centuries during which the land was governed by Romans, Moslems, Crusaders, Saracens and Turks did the people who lived in the land set up their own government. True, they fought over the land, they used the land, they abused the land. But only the Jew formed a government, drew the land to her bosom, loved her and made her to *"blossom like the rose"* (Isa. 35:1).

But what of the other Jews during all this time, most of whom had been scattered over the face of the earth? Had they fared better than their handful of counterparts who had stayed in the land?

In 1096, as many as 12,000 Jews were killed in Germany within three months. In 1290, Jews were banished from England. In 1306, Jews were banished from France. In 1348, Jews were blamed for the European plague. In 1492, under Ferdinand and Isabella, who wanted to make Spain a purely Catholic nation, the Spanish Inquisition was launched. Jews were required to convert and be baptized or they would be killed, imprisoned or driven out of Spain. It is estimated that 110,000 Jews had to flee.

As they were uprooted and driven from land to land, there was no haven at the end of the road, no protection along the way, and the ever-present danger of robbers and murderers. They were people without a land. It was rumored that the Jews killed infant Gentile children and used their blood in the observance of Passover. They were often required to wear a badge of identification. The women had to wear bells on the bottom of their dresses. Jews normally could not own ground, hold governmental office, attend the universities or work in most of the trades. Usury (the lending of money), merchandising, shoe repair and occasionally the managing of wealthy estates were among the few areas of gainful employment available to the Jew. In 1516, the first ghetto, where Jews were herded together and placed within a restricted area, was established in Venice. At the beginning of the nineteenth century, the largest Jewish population in the world was in Russia, and in 1883, they instituted the infamous pogroms. Over 500 Jewish villages were affected by over 1200 pogroms. More than 60,000 were killed and many times that number were wounded. It was these very pogroms which motivated this writer's grandparents to seek refuge in America. The government encouraged and then looked the other way as Russians attacked, harassed and robbed their Jewish neighbors. But, of course, this was nothing new. Through the centuries, when governments needed diversion to draw attention away from internal problems, the Jew was often a convenient scapegoat.

Between the years 1933 and 1945, the greatest attempt at genocide the world has ever known occurred. Under the depraved genius of Adolph Hitler, six million Jewish lives were snuffed out in the death camps, gas chambers and firing squads of the Third Reich. When many of the nations of the world had it within their power to save tens of thousands of fleeing European Jews, they took no action — refusing to increase immigration quotas and open their borders. Few even raised their voices in objection. For nineteen hundred years, "No Jews Wanted!" could have been written over most of the nations of the world.

What had they done? What was their crime? Why this never-ending persecution? To blame it, as so many have, on the Jewish national rejection of Christ is to acknowledge a total lack of understanding of the Word of God. Some have suggested that hatred of the sons of Jacob was the result of their strange religion. In a day of polytheism, they believed in the one true universal God. Their dietary laws, priesthood, temple worship, code of conduct and aloofness from other peoples all served to make them 'different' and defenseless.

Others have argued that abrasive character, excessive wealth and disproportionate influence are the root cause of hatred of the Jew. These at best are inadequate excuses and certainly not   defensible   answers.

The only accurate explanation for anti-Semitism is to be found in the fact that God chose Israel, through her greatest Son, to be the instrument for universal blessing and the ultimate defeat of Satan. To retaliate, the secret purpose of Satan, therefore, has always been to destroy the descendants of Abraham, Isaac and Jacob and thereby frustrate the divine plan for redemption of mankind. This is a foundational principle for understanding four thousand years of human history.

Satan has used his considerable power through the ages to attack God's chosen people through nations, movements and individuals. But in spite of satanically-inspired Crusades, pogroms, inquisitions, dispersions, ghettos, burnings and butcherings, the Jews somehow kept their identity. Their belief in the God of Abraham, Isaac and Jacob, their divine national destiny and the promise of a land given in perpetuity was strong enough to enable them to grasp the tail of one of the cyclones of history and ride that cyclone through two world wars back to their ancient homeland.

*And, somehow, in the midst of politics —
with a far greater Arab population in the Middle
East — with the increased interest in oil
— with movement toward the Second World
War — the "Balfour Declaration" and the
League of Nations mandate to Great Britain
were all but forgotten.*

10

Can These Bones Live?

Ezekiel looked on in stunned disbelief. Before him lay a valley of bones. The bones were *"very dry"*, indicating that the life they once supported was a long time dead. Nor was this a singular corpse, for the valley was *"full of bones"* (Ezek. 37:1-2). And as the prophet beheld the scene before him, God posed a question to His perplexed servant: *". . . can these bones live?"* (Ezek. 37: 3a). Everything normal, everything natural, everything pragmatic, everything humanistic, argued for a negative response. How could dry bones ever live? But, the prophet was a man of deep faith. His response was simply, *"O Lord God, thou knowest"* (Ezek. 37:3b). The prophet seemed to be saying, "These bones look dead to me. Humanly speaking, I don't see how they could possibly live. This is not a case of curing the sick, but of raising the dead. But Lord, you cast the stars into space — you spoke the world into existence — you fashioned man from the dust of the earth — if you want these bones to live, they can live." *"O Lord God, thou knowest."*

And, as the prophet prophesied as he was commanded, *". . . there was a noise and, behold, a shaking, and the bones came together, bone to its bone. And when I beheld, lo, the sinews and the flesh came up upon them, and the skin covered them above, but there was no breath in them"* (Ezek. 37:7-8).

That no one need ever question this miraculous scene, God himself gave the interpretation. The dry bones symbolized the dispersed Jews, driven from the Land of Promise (in 70 A.D. and again in 135 A.D.), scattered among the nations of the world and, as a nation, physically and spiritually dead — deep in the grave they lay (Ezek. 37:11). The noise, the shaking, the bones coming together, the sinews and the flesh coming upon them, spoke of Israel's resurrection and restoration to the land (Ezek. 36 - 37). But, this restoration would be in unbelief — there was no breath in them (Ezek. 37:8). The Bible is clear: Israel's physical restoration to the land must precede her spiritual regeneration in the land (Ezek. 37:14). They must return in unbelief to sign a covenant with the Antichrist (Dan. 9:24-27). As a remnant returned from the Babylonian captivity in three stages and over a period of about ninety-one years (Zerubbabel, 536 B.C.; Ezra 458 B.C.; Nehemiah, 445 B.C.), the present return is also in stages and covers an indefinite period of time. It will consummate in spiritual regeneration at Christ's return — God will breathe upon Israel — a nation will be born in a day (Isa. 66:8).

Rome governed Israel from 63 B.C. until 320; A.D. They were supplanted by the Byzantines, who stayed until defeated by the Arabs in 636. The Arabs continued to rule until unseated by the Seljuks in 1072. The "Christian" crusaders wrested control from the Seljuks in 1099, only to be defeated by the Mamlukes in 1187. They in turn fell prey to the Ottoman Turks in 1516, who ruled for four hundred years, until they were dethroned by the British in 1917. Each came seeking to possess the land of Abraham. But, as certainly as they entered they were spewed out. And, from 70 A.D. through all those centuries, the Jew, scattered among the nations of the world, lay in the grave — dead. The bones were very dry. Only an all-knowing and all-powerful God could ever have foretold and engineered Israel's return to her ancient homeland.

No one can with precision date the moment that the dry bones in Ezekiel's valley began to make "noise", but a logical starting point was 1897. The occasion was the First Zionist Congress convened at Basel, Switzerland. The luminary figure on that occasion was Dr. Theodore Herzl. He would later say, "At Basel I laid the foundation of the Jewish state. After five, or perhaps fifty years, everybody will realize it." Exactly fifty years later, in 1947, the United Nations would partition Palestine as a major step to establishing a Jewish homeland.

Herzl had been sent to Paris as a correspondent of a well-known Austrian newspaper. While there, he viewed repeated instances of anti-Semitism, culminating with the infamous trial of Alfred Dreyfus in 1894. Dreyfus was a captain on the general staff of the French Army — the only Jew to serve in this position. He was accused of giving secrets to the enemy and tried before a military court-martial. Although the evidence was overwhelming that Dreyfus was innocent, after two trials the "Jewish" captain was found guilty. Only after years of torture and imprisonment on Devil's Island was he exonerated of all charges lodged against him. But, the anti-Semitic furor which was fanned by the Dreyfus trial shocked Herzl and European Jewry. Angered and stirred, he wrote a pamphlet, **Der Judenstadt,** calling for a homeland for the wandering Jew. The First Zionist Congress was the result.

Max Nordau, one of the distinguished delegates, drafted a document which set forth Zionist aims. The opening statement is an accurate definition of what Zionism is. "Zionism," he wrote, "seeks to establish a home for the Jewish people in Palestine secured under public law." The movement was not without problems from the very beginning, both from within and without. Many Jews were vehemently opposed to a Jewish state, content where they were or fearful that attempts to establish a Jewish homeland would ignite new waves of anti-Semitism. And, among those who favored a new homeland, debate raged over where to locate it. Efforts to deal with the Ottoman Turks, who were in control of Palestine at the time, proved futile.

Alternate suggestions to establish the new state in places like Argentina, North America, the Sinai Peninsula and Uganda were made, examined and rejected. In the end the invisible, divine magnetism of Israel would prove irresistible. Only there could a truly Jewish state be forged. So formidable was the opposition – so unlikely its chances of success – that friends of Herzl suggested he visit a psychiatrist. Instead, he visited Baron Hirsch, a Jew who was a multimillionaire, and shared his plans. But, the rich Jew considered Herzl a mere visionary, a dreamer of dreams that would never be realized. Undaunted, he went to the Sultan of Turkey and offered to buy the land of Palestine, which was then under Turkish control. For Herzl's troubles, the Sultan presented him with three medals of honor – but no land.

Generally unknown is the fact that while some Jews were initially opposed to a Jewish homeland, many true believers sought to give support to what they understood to be a divine undertaking. In the Jewish Agency Building in Jerusalem is a large room which is a replica of Dr. Herzl's study. The appointments are original – his desk, a number of his chairs and the pulpit from which he spoke at the First Zionist Congress. On the wall is a framed photograph of his good friend, the Reverend Mr. Hechler, the chaplain of the British Embassy in Vienna.

It was this good friend who opened doors by introducing Herzl to prominent people in Europe, including the famous Grand Duke of Baden, who was the uncle of Emperor William II of Germany.

Also to be found in Herzl's study is his library. And, among these books is a very special Bible. It was presented to him by a Mr. A. Holland of Surrey, England, on August 24, 1900. On the flyleaf of the Bible the donor wrote, "See Ezekiel, chapters 36 to 39" (which speak glowingly of the resurrection of the land and the restoration of its people). On the second flyleaf Mr. Holland had written references to Isaiah 53 (which describes Messiah's death), Daniel 9:25-27 (which foretells the time of Messiah's death), and their New Testament fulfillment in Matthew, chapters 26 to 27. And, what is particularly meaningful to this writer are the words which were inscribed for the presentation to Dr. Herzl: "Kindly accept this Old and New Testament, His pure Word, from a lover of Israel, God's ancient people. May the God of Israel guide you and your helpers in the work of deliverance." Would to God, this characterized the views of more of His redeemed children today.

When the Turkish rule over Palestine fell to the British in 1917, it was General Allenby, a godly believer and lover of Israel, who captured the city of Jerusalem without firing a shot. In great humility, he dismounted and walked into the holy city, not wanting to ride as a conquering hero into the city over which His Savior and Lord would one day rule.

One day a group of Galilean farmers descended on a bank in Jerusalem. They wanted to borrow money to drain the swamp and malaria-infested Huleh Valley located a few miles north of the Sea of Galilee. The bank committee met — they considered the request — and turned it down. One of the farmers knew that the bank president was a Christian who believed the Bible. He directed him to Ezekiel 36:9 and read these words, *"For, behold, I am for you. . . ."* The Jewish farmer then asked the Christian banker, "What is the 'you' that God is referring to?" The banker acknowledged the "you" referred to the land of Israel. The farmer responded, "All we want to do is help God out. We need some money to drain the swamp and work the soil." The loan was approved and today the Huleh Valley stands as one of the breadbaskets of Israel.

The Hadassah Hospital in Jerusalem is perhaps the finest in the Middle East. Today, medicine is an advanced science in Israel. But, fifty years ago there were no hospitals in Israel, except for those which were staffed by Christians who treated both Jews and Arabs in the name of Jesus Christ.

Few informed people today can deny the quality, courage and dedication of the Israeli army. However, not as many realize that the man who initially trained the Israelis in guerrilla warfare and night fighting was a British officer. His name was Orde Wingate. He too was a godly believer. In one hand he carried a rifle, in the other a Bible. He took the Bible literally and believed that God means what He says and says what He means. Wingate was convinced that God intended that Palestine be a homeland for the Jew. Even today, in Israel Wingate is spoken of with great warmth and affection.

While there were forces that opposed Herzl and his dream for a Jewish homeland, there were those courageous souls among the Jewish people who stood with him.

One of them was Chaim Weizmann. More than any other man he, along with Herzl, was responsible for the modern state of Israel. He had worked earnestly for the cause of Zionism since his young manhood. During the latter part of the First World War, Britain and her allies were in the midst of a great crisis. The very outcome of the war itself was at stake. A chemical called acetone, used in the making of cordite, was in short supply. It was essential for the producing of explosives. Lloyd George, then the Minister of Munitions, contacted Chaim Weizmann, who was a brilliant chemist working at the University of Manchester. He conveyed Britain's need and the chemist rolled up his sleeves and went to work day and night. Within weeks, Weizmann developed a substitute for the scarce chemical. The day was saved for Britain and her allies. The British government, wanting to express its gratitude, asked Dr. Weizmann what they could do to show their appreciation. The response was, "Nothing for me, but for my people, a homeland in Palestine."

As soon as Lloyd George became Prime Minister, he conferred with Lord Balfour, who was the Foreign Secretary, concerning the request of the Jewish chemist who had rendered such valuable service to Great Britain. Both were favorably disposed to the Jewish cause. At least in part, this request was responsible for the historic "Balfour Declaration" of November 2, 1917. It stated:

> His Majesty's Government views with favor
> the establishment in Palestine of a national
> home for the Jewish people, and will use their
> best endeavors to facilitate the achievement
> of this object, it being clearly understood
> that nothing shall be done which may pre-
> judice the civil and religious rights of non-
> Jewish communities in Palestine, or the rights
> and political status enjoyed by Jews in any
> other country.

Twenty years earlier, delegates at the First Zionist Congress expressed their desire to "seek to establish a home for the Jewish people in Palestine SECURED UNDER PUBLIC LAW." With publication of the "Balfour Declaration", Great Britain, one of the world's most powerful nations, expressed agreement with and support for that goal. The bones which had begun to make a "noise" two decades earlier were now beginning to "shake and come together".

Shortly after World War I, the League of Nations was formed. In 1922, five years after the "Balfour Declaration", that international body gave a mandate to Great Britain to establish a homeland for the Jewish people. Now, "sinew and flesh" were beginning to cover those dead bones.

During the years that Herzl and his followers sought recognition of a Jewish state, other Jews fleeing persecution, or with idealistic dreams, returned by the thousands from Russia, Poland and other countries to the land promised to Abraham, Isaac and Jacob and their seed as an everlasting possession. What they found was a barren, desolate, malaria-infested, swampy land. Mark Twain, describing the area north of the Sea of Galilee more than ninety years ago, wrote, "There is not a solitary village throughout its whole extent – more than thirty miles in either direction. There are two or three small clusters of Bedouin tents, but not a single permanent habitation. One may ride ten miles hereabouts and not see any human being."

At first, the trees had been cut by invading armies so that other armies could not live off the land, and then with the introduction of the railroad, the Turks cut more trees to fuel the trains. In time, the topsoil, with no trees to hold it, was washed away by the rain. Used, abused and finally raped, the land was owned mostly by absentee landlords, most living in Syria. And, when the Jews began to return in successive waves of Aliyah (meaning to ascend), they bought land for what the absentee landlords thought was exorbitant profit. Literally thousands of these early pioneers died as they planted eucalyptus trees and drained the swamps. But still they came.

And somehow, in the midst of politics — with a far greater Arab population in the Middle East — with the increased interest in oil — with movement toward the Second World War — the "Balfour Declaration" and the League of Nations mandate to Great Britain were all but forgotten. In 1939, succumbing to Arab pressure, Britain published the infamous "White Papers" which restricted Jewish immigration to fifteen hundred people a month — less than a drop in the bucket — and this at a time when the Eastern European Jewish population was being decimated by Hitler.

Would the bones, which by this time had come together, were connected with sinew and covered with flesh, collapse under the weight of such pressure? During the Second World War, the Jews in Israel set aside their feud with England and fought on the side of the allies. Only after the war did the world come to know the enormity of the Nazi crimes against the Jews of Eastern Europe. Six million Jews   —   men, women and children — died in the death camps, ovens and before the firing squads of the Third Reich. And this not among the barbarians but within nations that called themselves "Christian". How accurate the words of God's spokesman, *"The heart is deceitful above all things, and desperately wicked; who can know it?"* (Jer. 17:9).

Following the war, survivors of the Holocaust, using whatever mode of transportation possible, tried to make their way to Israel. The British, rigidly enforcing the "White Papers", would capture Jews seeking to enter Israel and send them back to Europe or confine them on the island of Cyprus, allowing only fifteen hundred per month to enter Israel. But still the Jew came and, finally, unable to quell the disturbances between the Jew and Arab, Britain turned the matter over to the United Nations. Today, Great Britain is a morally, economically and militarily bankrupt nation. In the day Great Britain issued the "Balfour Declaration", she was probably the strongest nation in history. *"How are the mighty fallen!"* (2 Sam. 1:19, 27). She had a moral and legal right to help establish a homeland for the Jew, but because of political consideration she reneged on her promise. For nations and individuals, the Word of God still stands: *"And I will bless them that bless thee* [the Jew], *and curse him that curseth thee. . . "* (Gen. 12:3).

The thorny Jewish problem was placed into the lap of the United Nations. In November of 1947 they voted to partition Palestine and establish a homeland for the Jew. Two key factors in the outcome were world sympathy because of the Jewish atrocities in the Second World War and a favorable Russian vote — the latter, because many of the Jews in Israel were from Russia and the dramatically mistaken belief that the new nation would give Russia a toehold in the Middle East. The voting took only three minutes, but to world Jewry it seemed to stretch the entire nineteen hundred years of the exile.

An ancient Jewish sage once wrote,
If not here — where?
If not now — when?
If not you — who?
The place was Israel, the time had come, the people were the Jews.

Blatant Arab threats notwithstanding, on May 14, 1948 Ben Gurion, the nation's first Prime Minister, in an emotional speech declared Israel a free and independent nation among the nations of the world. The bones which Ezekiel saw prophetically twenty-five hundred years earlier had made a "noise", they "shook", the bones "came together", "the sinews and flesh" had come upon them, and now, at last, the bones *"stood up upon their feet. . ."* (Ezek. 37:10). But could she survive, in a hostile environment, surrounded by nations committed to her destruction?

On the 14th of May, 1948, Ben-Gurion, who would become Israel's first Prime Minister, declared Israel a nation. On the 15th, the last of the British forces withdrew. The same day, six Arab nations — Egypt, Syria, Transjordan, Lebanon, Saudi Arabia and Iraq — invaded Israel.

11

The Bush Burned and Was Not Consumed

With the United Nations resolution of November, 1947, Israel became a "paper" nation. Legally, Palestine was partitioned. The nations of the world had given Israel back a piece of the land that God had promised to Abraham and his posterity when He said, *". . . walk through the land in the length of it and in the breadth of it; for I will give it unto thee"* (Gen. 13:17). To be sure, what the United Nations gave was small — less than a fourth of the size which the British had proposed in the mandate — less square footage than the state of New Jersey. But it was something — a land — a home — a place to which the wandering Jew could return and be welcomed. But, could what was given in theory be sustained in practice? In 1948 there were only six hundred thousand Jews in all of Israel. The surrounding Arab nations had a combined population of over eighty million, and they threatened to drive the Jews into the Mediterranean Sea. There were only six months to prepare for the inevitable attack. The nearly one hundred thousand British troops who had kept a shaky, largely pro-Arab peace would then leave.

World leaders were largely agreed — if Israel declared herself a nation, the Arabs would attack and Israel would be stillborn. General George Marshall, American Secretary of State, counseled his friend, David Ben-Gurion, to bide his time until a more favorable political climate could develop for declaring Israel's nationhood. Ben-Gurion, later reflecting on the general's advice, said, ". . . For Marshall could not know what we knew — what we felt in our very bones: that this was our historic hour; if we did not live up to it, through fear or weakness of spirit, it might be generations or even centuries before our people were given another historic opportunity — if indeed we would be alive as a national group."

On the 14th of May, 1948, Ben-Gurion, who would become Israel's first Prime Minister, declared Israel a nation. On the 15th, the last of the British forces withdrew. The same day, six Arab nations — Egypt, Syria, Transjordan, Lebanon, Saudi Arabia and Iraq — invaded Israel. They approached like a fistful of fingers that would close together and pinch the life out of the infant state.

The invading armies had a carefully devised plan and a precise timetable. The Egyptians were to sweep up the coast from the south and then fork out. One force would take Jaffa-Tel Aviv along the Mediterranean Sea. The second force would join the Arab legion and converge on Jerusalem. From the east, Iraqi troops would race westward across Palestine toward the Mediterranean to slice Israel in half. In the north, the Syrians and Lebanese would join forces to secure Galilee and Haifa.

For the first month, battles raged up and down the land. The Jewish forces, initially without a tank, a fighter plane or a field gun, suffered heavy casualties. The situation looked very grim. Through the efforts of the United Nations, a truce went into effect on June 11th. It would only last until July 9th. But, it gave Israel a month's reprieve — it would prove to be all she needed.

Knowing that war was coming, Israeli agents were sent out to locate caches of military equipment. At the same time, Golda Meir, an amazing and courageous woman who would later become Prime Minister, was dispatched to America. Her assignment: raise five million dollars to purchase weapons. Born in Russia, brought to America as a child, she lived, was educated and taught school in Milwaukee, Wisconsin. As a young woman and a Zionist, she immigrated to Israel. Now back in America, the first night at a rally in New York she raised eleven million dollars — and ultimately she would raise fifty million. Word went out to Israel's agents to buy whatever equipment they could.

Now equipment began to trickle into the country. When the fighting resumed, the Arabs discovered a drastic turn of events. There is hardly a settlement in Israel that does not have its tales of tanks stopped at the gate with Molotov cocktails, of rifles snatched up for use from the hands of the dead, of fighting at ten-to-one odds — unembellished feats of individual and group heroism that would compare with the exploits of Joshua, Gideon and King David.

Egypt sent an armada of ships to shell the city of Tel Aviv located on the Mediterranean coast. Israel had no ships, no guns — she lay at the mercy of the attacking armada. Two young Israelis went aloft to meet the enemy — their plane a Piper Cub — their bombs handmade. The pilot was David Sprinzak, whose father would become the first Speaker of the Israeli Parliament. The bombardier was Mati Sukenik, whose father secured and deciphered the Dead Sea Scrolls. The little plane dove on the lead ship and hit it — the entire armada turned tail and fled — Tel Aviv was saved. But the plane crashed and both young men died.

A major Egyptian force was moving north through the

Negev. In its path stood a kibbutz (a communal farm) composed of nothing more than a row of cabins around a concrete water tower, in the open desert.

The kibbutz had seventy-five settlers, to which were added seventy more fighters. Their total arsenal consisted of eighty rifles, two machine guns and an antitank gun with five shells. Anticipating an attack, a complete underground fortress was built, staffed by a doctor and four nurses. Totally surrounded by the enemy, supplied only by a Piper Cub, with every aboveground building destroyed, the Negba Kibbutz defenders held out for six months, emerging victorious. On one day alone, June 2nd, six thousand shells fell on the surrounded garrison. Then came the major attack: seven Egyptian tanks, twelve armored cars, two thousand men, and overhead flying cover were two Arab-flown Spitfires. The battle lasted five hours. When the dust had cleared, six tanks nad been hit, one Spitfire shot down, and the Egyptians had pulled back.

A little more than a month later, Egypt renewed its attack. This time they were met head-on by a rugged group of jeep-mobilized commandos dubbed "Samson's Foxes". Within ten days, the dazed Egyptians would find their assault shattered, casualties high and much of their equipment in Jewish hands. One of those commando units was commanded by an eyepatched officer who would later become Chief of Staff — his name was Moshe Dayan.

At the southern end of the Sea of Galilee, where the lake empties into the Jordan River, stands the oldest and largest kibbutz in Israel. Its name is Degania. Combined Arab forces came against Degania with tanks, machine guns and soldiers. In bitter fighting, the Arab forces gained entrance to the colony, but the oldest settler urged the young men to hold on. Things looked desperate. As the tanks began to enter the compound, two young people, a boy and a girl about fifteen or sixteen years of age, were hidden in the bushes. They had crude, handmade weapons. They were bottles of phosphorus that burst into flame when the bottles were broken. One of these young people threw one of the Molotov cocktails right into a tank. The bottle burst — the tank caught fire. The attacking enemy, seeing the destruction of one tank and damage to three others, fled in disarray. The colony and city of Tiberias were saved and another attack blunted. The visitor to Israel can still see the tank at the entrance to the kibbutz left as a memorial.

In another major battle, Iraqi, Syrian and Transjordan forces came together to capture northern Israel and the major city of Haifa. It was at a Jewish colony near Mount Megiddo that the decisive battle took place. Once again, the Jews found themselves outgunned, outmanned, and surrounded. The besieged Jews had very few arms and had given up all hope of deliverance. Suddenly, there was a gap in the Arab lines. To this very day, no one has a human explanation for it. Jewish defense forces at once entered the colony through the gap to reinforce the beleaguered defenders. Stunned at this reversal, the Arabs withdrew their forces. This was the turning point in the battle for the Jezreel Valley and northern Israel.

All hostilities were concluded by January 7, 1949. The War of Independence was over. Israel was a nation — not only on paper, but in substance. Not only had she held on to the United Nations allocated land, but she captured additional territory in the north, south and central areas. It had been a long time coming — almost nineteen hundred years. And the final eight months had not been without great cost. Four thousand soldiers and two thousand civilians had given their last ounce of de

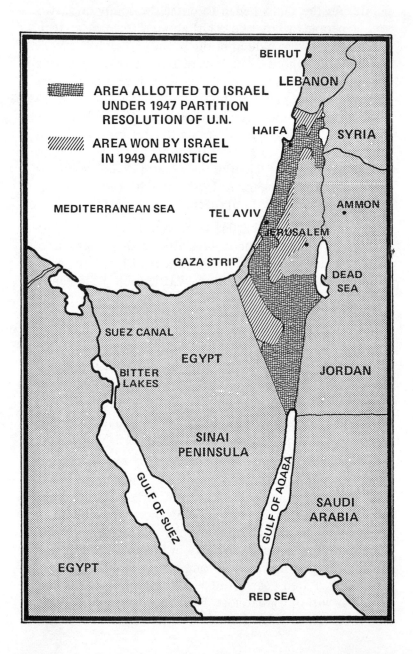

AREA ALLOTTED TO ISRAEL UNDER 1947 PARTITION RESOLUTION OF U.N.

AREA WON BY ISRAEL IN 1949 ARMISTICE

BEIRUT

LEBANON

HAIFA

SYRIA

MEDITERRANEAN SEA

TEL AVIV

AMMON

JERUSALEM

GAZA STRIP

DEAD SEA

SUEZ CANAL

EGYPT

JORDAN

BITTER LAKES

SINAI PENINSULA

GULF OF SUEZ

GULF OF AQABA

SAUDI ARABIA

EGYPT

RED SEA

votion. The financial drain on the young nation was staggering — five hundred million dollars.

In the calculations of the nuclear century, Israel is an insignificant piece of real estate. Her bridge is fragile; her highway narrow. And, to that insignificant and fragile land, Jews in great numbers from all over the world began to return. For almost three million Jews, something inside would say, "It's time to go home."

In 1956 the modern state of Israel found herself engaged in a second war. General Nasser was, in 1948, a colonel in the Egyptian army. He was defeated in battle near the very spot where David had defeated Goliath almost three thousand years earlier. Later, Nasser seized power in Egypt. Like Hitler, he wrote of how he would expand his sphere of influence and unite the Arab world. And like Hitler, the glue to solidify his aim would be hatred of the Jew. It was easy to suggest to the languishing refugees of Israel's War of Independence that, "You have been driven from your homes by the Jews!" A group of terrorists and murderers were trained to slip undetected into Israel to kill. Supplied and encouraged by Russia, who desperately wanted a foothold in the Middle East, Nasser seized the British-owned Suez Canal. An all-out attack on Israel was imminent. Ben-Gurion decided to strike at once and sent General Dayan into the Sinai. His troops destroyed terrorist bases and captured large stores of Soviet arms.

Within ten days, the Egyptian resistance was broken and Dayan penetrated to the Suez Canal, capturing the Red Sea port of Sharm El Sheikh and opening the Straits of Tiran to Israeli vessels. Under United Nations pressure, Israel withdrew, but the waterways were now open.

In June of 1967 Israel found herself in a squeeze play for the third time in nineteen years. A nation that wanted only peace, who preferred that her hardware be for farming not fighting, found this by-now-familiar cycle traumatic and disheartening. This time the antagonists were Syria, Jordan and Egypt. Launching a preemptive strike, Israel hit first. In six days it was all over. The war-making capabilities of the three aggressor nations were destroyed.

Israel captured the strategic Golan Heights in the northeast from Syria; the entire Sinai in the south from the Egyptians, and, most significantly, the Old City of Jerusalem and biblical Judea-Samaria (west bank) from Jordan. No battle in the history of mankind was more awesome. An observer put it this way: "By a feat of arms unparalleled in modern times, the Israelis, surrounded by enemies superior in quantity and quality of equipment and overwhelmingly superior in numbers, had fought a war on three fronts and not only survived, but won a resounding victory."

In 1948 Israel won an amazing battle for national survival against six invading armies. In 1956, when terrorists were sniping at her and the closing of the Suez Canal threatened to strangle the life out of her, she launched a daring campaign into the Sinai and emerged victorious. In 1967, in imminent danger of being attacked by three nations, she initiated a preemptive strike with such precision that the whole world was stunned. To the spiritually-discerning mind, it was the God of Israel who was behind these amazing victories.

But, following the Six Day War, Israel made a major mistake. She gloried not in what the God of her forefathers had done for her — but in what she thought she had done for herself. Israel was lifted up with pride, a pride of invincibility, of self-sufficiency. And so, on a quiet day in October, Israel found herself in another war.

It was Yom Kippur (the Day of Atonement), October 6, 1973. Egypt and Syria launched a massive coordinated attack — Egypt across the Suez Canal and Syria over the Golan Heights.

The Israeli intelligence-gathering capability is among the best in the world. Literally hundreds of warnings were received from secret agents telling of the impending attack — some giving the very hour. American intelligence confirmed the attack forty-eight hours in advance. But, it was as though the Jewish leaders had a veil placed over their eyes — they refused to heed the repeated and urgent warnings. Jewish leadership was either convinced the Arabs would not attack or confident that they could handily repeal any infringement on her sovereignty.

They chose not to launch a preemptive strike, as they did in 1967, fearful of worldwide condemnation as an aggressor; they chose not to mobilize lest it be a false alarm and they needlessly disrupt the economy; they chose not to disrupt the religious holidays and offend the religious Jews — amazingly, they did nothing.

With perhaps as many as two thousand tanks at the ready, the Syrians started over the Golan Heights to attack a totally unprepared enemy. Simultaneously, the Egyptians, in a massive show of strength, crossed the Suez Canal to be met by less than five hundred Israeli soldiers.

Within hours the Israeli government realized the magnitude of the attack. Israel was fighting for her very survival. Her planes took to the skies and tried gallantly to stem the tide. But, Russian-built Sam 7 ground-to-air missiles formed an "umbrella-like" protection over the advancing armies. In air-to-air combat, it was no contest — the Israelis were clearly superior. But, they had little defense against the ground-to-air missiles which kept them at bay. And, newly-deployed antitank weapons were taking a heavy toll. In the early days of the war, the situation looked desperate.

According to the article, "How Israel got the Bomb" in **Time** magazine, April 12, 1976, Moshe Dayan, the Chief of Staff, requested permission of Prime Minister Golda Meir to arm their atomic bombs. They came out of storage silos and were moved to a number of airfields to be armed and ready if needed. Russia, seeing what Israel was doing, began to ship nuclear devices to Alexandria. Former President Nixon, informed of the Russian activity, called a red alert for the American armed forces worldwide. Super-power confrontation and atomic war were distinct possibilities.

And, at that moment, a brilliant Israeli tank commander was able to break through the Egyptian advance and cross the Suez Canal. His troops fanned out and destroyed the Sam 7 missile sights. The Israeli planes now controlled the skies. In the following days, in what was one of history's largest tank battles, the Egyptian mechanized units were destroyed on the sands of the Sinai Desert. Jewish troops continued to cross the Canal and encircled the Egyptian Third   Army.

At the same time, there was a dramatic change in the battle for the Golan Heights. Acts of heroism abounded and gave Israel a chance to mobilize her forces.

Among the most conspicuous were the exploits of a young Israeli, Zvi Greengold. He was on leave when news of the outbreak of fighting reached him. Hitchhiking north, he arrived at headquarters and asked for a command. He was given four tanks and sent into the battle. Over the next thirty hours, Zvi Greengold would reap havoc on the enemy. When other tanks in his command were destroyed, he fought alone, engaging one of the main thrusts of the Syrian advance. Through the night he darted in and out among the hills to destroy enemy tanks then would quickly melt into the night. His tank was hit and set afire. Zvi flung himself to the ground, wounded and suffering burns on his arms and face. Still, the lieutenant commandeered a passing Israeli tank and continued his war. Zvi Greengold, son of survivors of the Holocaust, had single-handedly, according to figures given by his officers, destroyed sixty Syrian tanks. This author personally interviewed the officer who was in charge of refueling and rearming the tanks. In detail, he verified the story. Such exploits are reminiscent of the days of Samson.

In time both the Syrian and Egyptian invasions were repulsed — the entire atmosphere of the war changed. The atomic bombs went back into storage silos — the Russians unloaded their paratroopers and the American armed forces were taken off red alert. Israel now had the capability of destroying both Cairo, Egypt and Damascus, Syria. But, within forty-eight hours, the United Nations called for a cease-fire. America feared that Russia would have to directly intervene, and therefore put pressure on Israel to cease fire. While Israel was fighting for her life, few nations protested and the United Nations took little action; but when the tide of battle miraculously changed, the United Nations acted with great dispatch.

For Israel, for the moment at least, the day was saved. It would take her some months to realize that the Yom Kippur War was, in reality, a victory. But, the pride which had characterized her after the 1967 Six Day War was no longer present.

Long centuries ago, Moses saw a bush that burned and was not consumed. He said, *"I will now turn aside and see this great sight, why the bush is not burnt"* (Ex. 3:3). The burning bush which Moses beheld needed no hot flame to reduce it quickly into a heap of white ashes. In all probability the region was arid and dry, the bush scorched and withered, its leaves dead and limp, its branches dry and sapless. The lapping flames should have made speedy work .of such a bush. But the thorn was not consumed; no branch or twig or leaf was even scorched or singed.

The visual object lesson was clear and concise. Though every normal indication argued for the annihilation of the thorn bush, it was miraculously and supernaturally preserved. At that same moment the Hebrew race was enslaved down in Egypt; 'stunted' because of depravations; 'thorny', with no apparent value; in the crucible of 'fiery' affliction. Every normal indication argued for extinction — but like the thorn bush, that people would be miraculously and supernaturally preserved. And like the thorn bush, Jehovah would speak from the midst of her to the peoples of the world. That day is fast approaching.

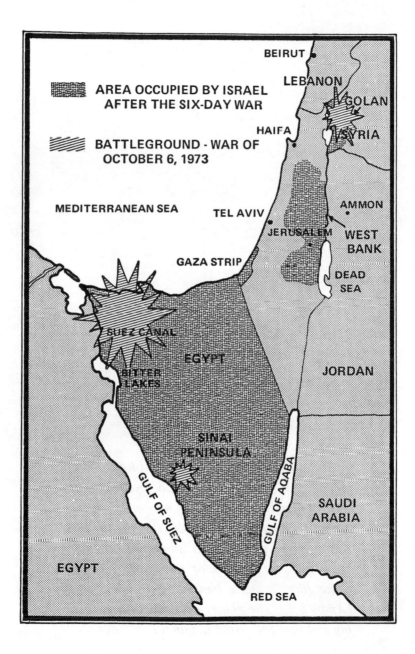

And, the insanity of the present hour is that mankind is racing madly and unerringly toward Armageddon — by his actions he is hastening its arrival. In the words of the Prophet Amos, as he pronounced imminent judgment on Israel, the nations of the world have become like ". . . a basket of summer fruit" (Amos 8:1). The planet Earth is rotting, smelling and ripe for divine judgment.

12

Armageddon: The Gathering Storm

Situated in the north central part of Israel fifteen
miles inland from the Mediterranean seacoast and ten
miles south of Nazareth, where the Son of God grew to
manhood, is a small hill called, for more than three thousand years, Mount Megiddo. The stranger passing by
would scarcely give attention to this protruding mound
of dirt. There is nothing of grandeur associated with its
appearance. Nearby, and in clear view, are Mounts Tabor,
Gilboa and Carmel, all considerably larger and higher
than Mount Megiddo. Immediately to the northeast is
the Plain of Esdraelon (Greek) or Jezreel (Hebrew). This
plain is fourteen miles wide and twenty miles long. In
marked contrast to the stranger unimpressed by Mount
Megiddo, rulers and military leaders have for thousands
of years understood its paramount, strategic importance.

Treasure-laden caravans and marching armies, moving
north from Egypt and the Nile or south from Syria and
the Euphrates, could choose one of two possible routes
to travel. One, called the KINGS HIGHWAY, passed
through the arid, semi-desert area of the Negev and the
rugged, inhospitable mountains of eastern Israel. The alternative was the VIA MARIS, or WAY OF THE SEA.
This level coastline route, with its many wells and
springs, was far safer and easier to travel for both man
and beast. For this reason, the Via Maris was one of the

major highways of the ancient world. Midway through
the Plain of Sharon in western Israel, the main branch
of the Via Maris broke away from the coastline and cut
through the Carmel Mountains (the Aruna Pass) and into the Plain of Esdraelon. An army garrisoned atop
Mount Megiddo would be able to see invading forces still
far off and could deploy troops to intercept them at a
point of their own choosing. An added advantage was an
ingenious water shaft sunk 120 feet deep and connected
by a tunnel 215 feet long to springs outside the walls.
This allowed its defenders to hold out under an extended
siege. The Bible repeatedly makes reference to this battlefield.

It was here that Deborah and Barak defeated the
Canaanites (Jud. 4 - 5); that Gideon and his band
of three hundred triumphed over the Midianites (Jud.
7); that King Saul was slain in the battle with the
Philistines (1 Sam. 31:8); that King Ahaziah was
slain by Jehu (2 Ki. 9:27); and that good King
Josiah was slain during an invasion by the Egyptians (2
Ki. 23:29 - 30).

Mount Megiddo has been a chosen place of encamp-
ment for most of the major battles in Israel for more
than thirty centuries. Egyptians, Hittites, Israelites,
Philistines, Assyrians, Persians, Greeks, Romans, Crusaders, Turks and the British have pitched their tents on
the Plain of Esdraelon to do battle. So crucial was control of Mount Megiddo that King Solomon fortified it
and stabled horses and chariots there to literally "cut
off at the pass" any invading army moving toward Israel
from the north or east. Napoleon, one of history's towering military leaders, called the area surrounding Mount
Megiddo the world's most natural battlefield. More battles have been fought there than on any other piece of
real estate in the world.

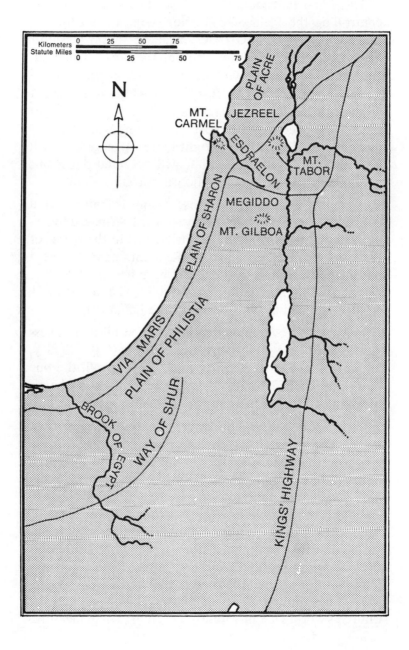

This important mount, which sits like a silent sentinel controlling the Plain of Esdraelon, comes from the Hebrew words HAR MEGIDDO, meaning Mount Megiddo. And, from "Har Megiddo" comes the word which has become synonymous with catastrophic, climactic judgment — ARMAGEDDON. But, Armageddon is important today, not because of past wars which have been fought there — but because the most devastating war of all human history is still to be fought there. Armageddon will be the final stage upon which will be acted out man's inhumanity to man and rebelliousness against God.

And, the insanity of the present hour is that mankind is racing madly and unerringly toward Armageddon — by his actions he is hastening its arrival. In the words of the Prophet Amos, as he pronounced imminent judgment on Israel, the nations of the world have become like ". . . *a basket of summer fruit"* (Amos 8:1). The planet Earth is rotting, smelling and ripe for divine judgment.

In America, government has lost its credibility, business has lost its integrity, hard work has lost its dignity, morality has lost its nobility and, worst of all, the one thing that could have salvaged the present hour, the expression of TRUE Christianity, has lost its vitality.

Today few believe government, only the naive trust business, people want more and more for doing less and less, and ethical standards are no longer fashionable. As a result, political paralysis, economic chaos, military weakness and moral transgression — these are not ominous clouds on tomorrow's horizon but today's stark realities. America has known unprecedented blessing because she has, as no other nation in history, opened her borders to the wandering Jew and from her shores sent missionaries to the far-flung corners of the earth. When things get bad, she will begin to persecute the sons of Jacob and halt the Church's worldwide missionary program. These measures can be guaranteed to hasten America's downward spiral. Some will scoff at such statements — they will one day soon see how accurate they are.

And, if the situation is grave in America, world events offer no encouragement. The Russian bear has fully awakened out of her hibernation. Now with an insatiable appetite, no longer satisfied with simply encouraging discontent in far-off places, she has begun to rumble south toward the oil-rich Persian Gulf and warm water ports in the Indian Ocean. Her strategy is simple: control the world oil flow and bring the technologically-advanced nations to their knees — not for prayer but capitulation.

China, with her teeming millions, has in recent years begun a crash program of modernization. Now a world power to be reckoned with, the people of that land must one day break out of restrictive borders. The purpose will be to provide "bread" for her masses and to spread her particular brand of godless Communism.

The Arab-Muslim world, intoxicated by its new wealth and power and with a thirst to propagate its Islamic faith, can be reasonably expected to be aroused and incited into a "holy war" at any propitious time. There is historical precedent to suggest just such an action.

Among the newly emerging and third world nations, there is a growing, fierce determination to gain independence and to become part of the "have's" instead of the "have not's". They chafe at the fact that America, possessing eight percent of the world's population, uses thirty percent of the world's energy. It is among these nations that revolution and terrorism incubate, grow and thrive.

And, amid all of this, the power and economic base in the Western World is shifting from America to Western

Europe and the Mediterranean World. Now well under-
way is a conglomeration of nations that will become a
"United States of Europe". Ten nations will ultimately
be involved, corresponding to the ten toes of the image
of Daniel, chapter 2, and the ten horns of the fourth
beast of Daniel, chapter 7. Nine nations have been a
part of the Common Market community for some time,
including France, West Germany, Italy, Britain, Luxem-
bourg, Belgium, The Netherlands, Ireland and Denmark.
The tenth, Greece, will be formally admitted in January,
1981. Official representatives to this body have already
been elected. Among other things, a unified monetary system is being developed and tariffs between member nations can reasonably be expected to be lifted in the fore-
seeable future. It is from within this Western Confedera-
tion of nations that a man will rise to great power and
dominance. The Bible variously describes this individual
as the *"little horn"* (Dan. 7:8), the *"man of sin"* (2 Th.
2:3), *"the son of perdition"* (2 Th. 2:3), the *"antichrist"*
(2 Jn. 7), and the *"beast . . . out of the sea"* (Rev. 13:1).

Further, the Bible teaches that while these geopoliti-
cal alliances are being forged, there will be a growing
atmosphere characterized by disintegration of the family
unit (2 Tim. 3:2-3a), lawlessness (2 Tim. 3:3b-4) and
increased religion without reality (2 Tim. 3:5). One
would be hard pressed to more accurately describe the
national, political and moral trends of the present hour
— the inspired penman did so more than nineteen hundred years ago.

The planet Earth is a powder keg — the fuse has been
lit — an explosion is coming. No one can with certainty
predict the time. But, the fact that so many of the pieces
of the prophetic puzzle are falling into place strongly
suggests that the explosion cannot be far off.

What are the salient features leading to Armageddon

that may be reasonably expected? Next on the prophetic calendar is the Rapture of the true Church — the sudden, unannounced snatching up into the clouds of the bride of Christ (1 Th. 4:13-18). This will be followed by a seven-year peace covenant which the Antichrist — ruler of the United States of Europe, will make with Israel (Dan. 9:24-27). During the first three and one-half years, he will be busy consolidating his power. Near the middle of this "Tribulation" period, an invasion will be launched into the Middle East. The major antagonist will be Russia coming, as she does, from the far north of Israel (Ezek. 38:15, 19) and further identified by the terms Magog (the ancient Scythians of south-central Russia, according to the first century Jewish historian Josephus); Meschech (probably modern-day Moscow in western Russia); and Tubal (probably modern-day Tobolsk in eastern Russia). Further, the phrase *"chief prince"* (Ezek. 38:2) would be better translated "Prince of Rosh" and should be understood to be the ancestral name of present-day Russia.

Allied with her will be Persia, whose name was changed as recently as 1935 to Iran. This Russian and Iranian alliance had been proclaimed by godly Bible teachers long before the pro-Western Shah of Iran was deposed in 1979. When the Prophet Ezekiel wrote, the Persian World included modern-day Iran, Iraq and Afghanistan. Therefore, it is possible that these nations will be in the Russian camp. Cush and Put (usually identified as modern-day Ethiopia and Libya in North Africa and presently under strong Russian influence) will also be involved in this coming invasion (Ezek. 38:5). Other nations identified as being allied with Russia include Gomer (the Germanic peoples of Eastern Europe) and Togarmah (modern-day Turkey, Ezek. 38:6). Most of these nations are now in proper alignment.

Israel is described at this time as a *"land of unwalled villages . . . having neither bars nor gates"* (Ezek. 38:11). In the day in which the prophet wrote, walls were a city's main line of defense. An unwalled city was easy prey for any army so inclined to attack. Today, Israel is an armed camp. A disproportionately high percentage of her budget goes toward defense, and both men and women are drafted at age eighteen. But, after the Antichrist makes a covenant to protect Israel, arms expenditures will be redirected to improve the standard of living and she will become an *"unwalled village"*.

This author has discussed the coming Russian invasion of Israel with leaders in the highest echelon of Israeli government. Those spoken to were familiar with Ezekiel 38 - 39 and believed it to describe a Russian attack. But, with a shrug of the shoulder and a sense of futility, they suggested with wistful thinking that "perhaps the battle the prophet described has already been historically fulfilled." But even as they spoke, they knew no historical event met the criteria of Ezekiel's still-to-be-fulfilled prophecy.

Two reasons for the attack are given: first, *"To take a spoil"* (Ezek. 38:12) — mineral wealth of the Dead Sea, Middle East oil, agricultural capability and geographic military importance — these are among the spoils referred to. The second reason given for the attack is to deliberately harm the land of Israel and its people (Ezek. 38:12b). Godless, Satanically-empowered Communism takes no pleasure in the Jewish people through whom Christ and the Bible were given to the world.

This invasion by Russia and her allies will not succeed. Most of the invading army will be destroyed by God on the mountains of Israel (Ezek. 39:2-4). So complete will be the slaughter that it will take the people of Israel seven months to bury the dead and cleanse the land (Ezek. 39:12). Russia has said that she would bury the West, but God has said that He is going to bury Russia.

While the view expressed above places the Russian invasion of Israel after the Rapture of the Church and during the first half of the Tribulation period, it should be understood that an increasing number of competent teachers locate this battle near the end of this present age and before the Church is raptured.

A second invasion of the Promised Land is described in Daniel, chapter 11. This series of battles will culminate at Armageddon. A coordinated attack will be launched against Israel by Egypt and the king of the South, and Syria and the king of the North (Dan. 11:40). Such an attack against Israel will be seen as an attack against the Antichrist, since he has entered into a covenant to protect Israel. In response, he will launch a direct counter-attack into the Middle East (Dan. 11:43). While engaged in battle with Egypt, Ethiopia and Libya in North Africa, tidings from the East – China and probably Japan – and the North – the remnants of the earlier defeated Russian army – will trouble him (Dan. 11:44). The Antichrist will reverse direction and rush to repulse this new threat. The Eastern army alone will field more than two hundred million men (Rev. 9:16). Today, China with its more than nine hundred million people is capable of fielding just such an army. This campaign will involve major armies from the North, East, South and West. The Bible simply says, *"And he [God] gathered them together into a place called in the Hebrew tongue Armageddon"* (Rev. 16:16). Although the pivotal point will be Armageddon, the total battlefield will stretch for hundreds of miles. The Prophet Zechariah wrote, *"For I will gather all nations against Jerusalem to battle; and the city shall be taken, and the houses rifled, and the women ravished; and half of the city shall go forth into captivity, and the residue of the people shall not be cut off from the city. Then shall the Lord go forth, and fight against those nations, as when he fought in the day of battle"* (Zech. 14:2-3).

It's for that reason that the Lord told His disciples that the Jews living at that time should flee, *"For then shall be great tribulation, such as was not since the beginning of the world to this time, no, nor ever shall be. And except those days should be shortened, there should no flesh be saved . . . "* (Mt. 24:21-22). But, those days will be shortened by the direct intervention of the Lord Jesus Christ. The beloved Apostle John described that scene this way:

> *And I saw heaven opened and, behold, a white horse; and he that sat upon him was called Faithful and True, and in righteousness he doth judge and make war. His eyes were like a flame of fire and on his head were many crowns; and he had a name written, that no man knew, but he himself. And he was clothed with a vesture dipped in blood; and his name is called The Word of God. And the armies that were in heaven followed him upon white horses, clothed in fine linen, white and clean. And out of his mouth goeth a sharp sword, that with it he should smite the nations, and he shall rule them with a rod of iron; and he treadeth the winepress of the fierceness and wrath of Almighty God. And he hath on his vesture and on his thigh a name written, KING OF KINGS, AND LORD OF LORDS.*
> *Revelation 19:11-16*

Armageddon will be the final judgment of the nations because of their persecution of Israel (Joel 3:2), their sinfulness (Rev. 19:15), and their godlessness (Rev. 16: 9). Armageddon will be a vivid commentary on the biblical principle, *"Be not deceived, God is not mocked, for whatever a man* [or a nation] *soweth, that shall he also reap"* (Gal. 6:7).

And what of beloved America, "the land of the free and the home of the brave", during these earth-shattering events? She is not mentioned in the Bible. There is nothing to indicate that America will be part of the European ten-nation community of the West, though it must be said that some gifted teachers take this view. More likely, she will have been neutralized by war or will have collapsed under the weight of her own debauchery and corruption. As a third-class power, she will play no significant or identifiable role in the end-time events. These are not pleasant thoughts for those of us who dearly love America.

But, we cannot hide our faces from the clear and dramatic downward spiral of America at the present hour. Perhaps – just perhaps – God's people, through fervent prayer and genuine repentance, can slow her descent, but ultimate judgment cannot be averted.

Mankind need not succumb to total despair – there is light at the end of the tunnel – the dark night of Armageddon will revolve into the glorious day of Christ's millennial kingdom.

These unconditional promises, which God gave to King David and Mary, the mother of the Lord, of an eternal throne and kingdom through their seed, have never been historically fulfilled. They await implementation at the establishment of Christ's earthly kingdom. An immutable God does not break His promise.

13

Utopia at Last: God's Golden Age

The King is coming — make no mistake about it. An occasional bumper sticker announces it, many Christians anticipate it, the world desperately needs it, and the Bible authoritatively declares it. But — the King has come before.

Long centuries ago, wise men came from the East inquiring, *"Where is he that is born King of the Jews?. . ."* (Mt. 2:2), and in connection with the King's first coming, the inspired penman wrote, *". . . when the fullness of the time was come, God sent forth his Son. . ."* (Gal. 4: 4). There was no shabby planning here; everything was right on schedule.

The second coming of the Lord Jesus Christ will be no less precise. At His first coming, the Lamb died for the world's sin. At His second coming, the Lion will deliver the world from the ravages of sin (Heb. 9:28) and establish a thousand-year kingdom (Rev. 20:4).

In that day, unfulfilled prophecies will be fulfilled (those prophecies which relate to the King and kingdom); unexplained ceremonies will be explained (those ceremonies that relate to the Priest and priesthood); and unsatisfied longings will be satisfied (longings embodied in King David's heart cry, *"As the hart panteth after the water brooks, so panteth my soul after thee. . ."*, Ps. 42:1).

The poems of the poet, the songs of the musician, the novels of the author — the collective expressions of centuries of longings for a golden age will be realized — not through human effort, but by direct divine intervention.

The need for that day is CRUCIAL. The character of that day is GLORIOUS. And, the conclusion of that day will be TRIUMPHANT.

It is a **crucial** day because of the need to execute Satan. At the fall of Adam and Eve, Satan usurped man's right to rule as king of the earth. He is, the Bible declares, the *"god of this age"* (2 Cor. 4:4); he is the *"prince of the power of the air"* (Eph. 2:2). Awesomely, the Bible states that *"the whole world lieth in wickedness"* (literally, the wicked one, 1 Jn. 5:19); that is, in a semi-conscious stupor without even being aware of their situation. But, one day soon, the promised *"seed of the woman"* is going to recapture man's lost destiny as king of the earth. It was a man, Adam, who forfeited man's right to rule. It will be a Man, the God-Man, who will recapture it. As the Lamb of God, Jesus defeated Satan; as the Lion of Judah, Jesus will execute him. Satan will be chained and inoperative during Christ's thousand-year reign (Rev. 20:1-3).

It is a **crucial** day because of the need to substantiate the Lord's messianic claim. In the Old Testament there were three official offices — prophet, priest and king. The prophet was God's spokesman to the people; the priest, in contrast, was the people's representative before God; and the king was God's vice-regent, ruling over the people in civil affairs. Every need of the human heart could be met through those three offices. To the question, "In this confused, tumbling-out-of-control world in which I live, is there any objective truth in which I can trust and place my life?", the response given is, "Yes, hear God's Prophet." To the question, "Is there any way that a vile sinner like me can find acceptability before a holy God who is a consuming fire?", again the answer is, "Yes, through God's Priest." To the question, "Will righteousness, justice and peace ever become a reality upon the earth?", once more the answer is, "Yes, through the divinely-appointed King." During His first advent, Jesus was a prophet — He was God's spokesman to the people. During the last week of His life, He functioned as a priest offering the sacrifice to God and then turning around to be the only acceptable sacrifice. An infinite God required a sacrifice of infinite worth, and only Jesus would do. When He returns to the earth the second time, He will return as a legitimate heir, to a legitimate throne, over a legitimate people. His coming kingly ministry is absolutely essential to substantiate His messianic claim.

It is a **crucial** day, for it demonstrates God's faithfulness to His Word. To David God said,

> *And when thy days be fulfilled, and thou shalt sleep with thy fathers, I will set up thy seed after thee, which shall proceed out of thine own body, and I will establish his kingdom . . . And thine house and thy kingdom shall be established forever before thee; thy throne shall be established forever.*
>
> *2 Samuel 7:12, 16*

And to Mary, the mother of the Lord, the Angel Gabriel spoke these words:

> *And, behold, thou shalt conceive in thy womb, and bring forth a son, and shalt call his name JESUS. He shall be great, and shall be called the Son of the Highest; and the Lord God shall give unto him the throne of his father, David.*
>
> *Luke 1:31-32*

These unconditional promises which God gave to King David and Mary, the mother of the Lord, of an eternal throne and kingdom through their seed, have never been historically fulfilled. They await implementation at the establishment of Christ's earthly kingdom. An immutable God does not break His promise.

And, what a **glorious** day that will be. It will be a day of theocracy (Rev. 19:15-16). God, in the person of the Lord Jesus Christ, will rule directly over the affairs of men. And the curse placed upon the earth by the fall will be lifted. The average life span will be dramatically increased (Isa. 65:20). The earth will give her unhindered bounty (Isa. 35:1-2). There will be no more war, for the weapons of warfare will be fashioned into tools for farm implementation (Isa. 2:4). *"The wolf also shall dwell with the lamb, . . . and a little child shall lead them"* (Isa. 11:6). Peace (Isa. 11:1-5) and holiness and justice (Isa. 9:6-7) will characterize His glorious reign. What the earth could have been — would have been, had sin not entered through man's disobedience will be fully displayed.

The conclusion of that day will be one of absolute **triumph.** Satan will seek one final time to rebel against God and His Anointed. He will not succeed. His rebellion will be short-lived, and He will be forever consigned to eternal imprisonment and condemnation (Rev. 20:10) — never again to work his wiles against the heirs of God's grace.

That day will end with the Great White Throne Judgment, where God will judge unrepentant mankind in holiness and with justice.

"Be sure, your sins will find you out" is not some meaningless, impotent cliche; *". . . whatever a man soweth, that shall he also reap"* (Gal. 6:7). Here is an absolute law of life. If a man sows to the flesh, he will reap to the flesh; if he sows to the Spirit, he will reap to the Spirit (Gal. 6:8). To the unrepentant, this strikes terror to the heart. For the redeemed, it is a principle of unsurpassing comfort and further evidence of the intrinsic eternal perfections of God.

Two thousand years ago, wicked men took the Lord of glory, the Creator of all things, the Sovereign of the universe — they tried Him unjustly, crucified Him unmercifully, turned their backs, rubbed their hands, walked away and said, "We are done with Him!" But no one is done with Christ.

14

The Great White Throne Judgment

The final, climactic event of human history is called the Great White Throne Judgment (Rev. 20:11). The words themselves reflect the solemnity of the occasion. "Great" suggests power, "white" speaks of holiness and justice, and "throne" implies royalty and accountability. This judgment scene is the doorway between the literal thousand-year reign of Christ on earth which preceded it and the eternal state into which it unfolds on the other side. Once its threshold is crossed, the eternal destiny of the soul is irreversibly fixed. It is, therefore, a most somber, sober, sacred event.

But, who will participate in this judgment? Ancient Jewish sages suggested that there would be two individuals who would, in a special sense, be the Messiah of God. And, they gave names to these two individuals. One they called Messiah Son of Joseph – the other, Messiah Son of David. The first would suffer like Joseph, who was rejected by his brethren and sold into slavery. The second would rule in great power and be bedecked in glory like David, Israel's greatest king. Doubtless, this Talmudic concept of Messiah came from the fact that in the Scriptures of Israel there are portraits of a Messiah who would suffer (Ps. 22; Isa. 53) and reign (Ps. 24; Isa. 11).

In many respects, these ancient scholars were so close and yet tragically so far in their understanding of the Word of God. The inspired penmen were not describing two distinct Messiahs — one who would suffer and another who would reign. Rather, they were introducing one Messiah who would come to earth two times — the first time to suffer and die, and a second time to rule and reign. It is the bodily resurrection of Christ which makes possible the future coming of Him who has already come.

Henry Wadsworth Longfellow clearly understood the implications of this truth. War had been raging. His son had been wounded. The Christmas bells seemed to be mocking. And he wrote:

> *I heard the bells on Christmas day*
> *Their old familiar carols play,*
> *And wild and sweet the words repeat*
> *Of peace on earth, good will to men.*
>
> *I thought how, as the day had come,*
> *The belfries of all Christendom*
> *Had rolled along the unbroken song*
> *Of peace on earth, good will to men.*
>
> *And in despair I bowed my head:*
> *"There is no peace on earth," I said,*
> *"For hate is strong, and mocks the song*
> *Of peace on earth, good will to men."*
>
> *Then pealed the bells more loud and deep;*
> *"God is not dead: nor doth He sleep;*
> *The wrong shall fail, the right prevail,*
> *With peace on earth, good will to men."*
>
> *Till ringing, singing on its way*
> *The world revolved from night to day —*
> *A voice, a chime, a chant sublime*
> *Of peace on earth, good will to men!*

The Christmas bells tolled out the peace purchased by

the Lamb at His first coming, but which will be fully implemented and experienced through the Lion at His second coming. One day there will be peace on earth to men of good will. Nor was the Apostle Peter unfamiliar with this truth, for he wrote of *". . . the sufferings of Christ, and the glory that should follow"* (1 Pet. 1:11).

Two thousand years ago, wicked men took the Lord of glory, the Creator of all things, the Sovereign of the universe — they tried Him unjustly, crucified Him unmercifully, turned their backs, rubbed their hands, walked away and said, "We are done with Him!" And down through the centuries, multitudes have emulated their attitude by rejecting the Son of God. But in reality, nobody is done with the Lord Jesus Christ. He said, concerning His crucifixion, *"And I, if I be lifted up from the earth, will draw all men unto me"* (Jn. 12:32). The Apostle Paul wrote, *". . . every knee should bow. . . and . . . every tongue should confess that Jesus Christ is Lord, to the glory of God, the Father"* (Phil. 2:10-11).

Every human being who has ever lived will encounter Christ. The only issue open to man is where he chooses to meet Him — at Calvary as the Lamb of God who takes away the sin of the world, or at the Great White Throne as the Lion of the tribe of Judah who will judge in absolute holiness.

At Calvary, men confront the silence of the One who when *". . . brought as a lamb to the slaughter. . . openeth not his mouth"* (Isa. 53:7). At the Great White Throne, they will encounter the roaring of the Lion. At Calvary, men appear clothed in the righteousness provided by Christ, at the Great White Throne men stand before Him clothed in their self-righteousness. At Calvary there is grace, at the Great White Throne unbending laws.

If a man meets the Lamb at Calvary, he will not meet

122 • Not Without Design

the Lion at the Great White Throne. If he chooses to by-
pass Calvary, he cannot avoid the Great White Throne.
No man will participate in both judgments.

But, who is the Judge? And what is the basis of the
judgment? And, further, what will the judgment be?

The beloved Apostle John wrote, *"And I saw a great
white throne, and him that sat on it . . ."* (Rev. 20:11).
John saw the Judge. He is none other than the Lord
Jesus Christ. And, He is far removed in personality from
the description in the little Christmas chorus, "Little
Jesus, meek and mild". Because He is all-powerful, this
will be the supreme court of the ages — there will be no
higher court to which a man can appeal. The verdict will
be unalterable and final. Because He is all over all the
time, there will be no circumstantial evidence — the
deeds that men have done all their days will be known by
the Judge. Because He is all-knowing, even the very
thoughts which the mind has entertained will be open
before His gaze. The awesomeness of this is better understood if it be remembered that as a man *"thinketh
in his heart, so is he. . ."* (Prov. 23:7). The Judge will
also be perfect in holiness. He is *"a consuming fire"*
(Heb. 12:29). — He is *"light, and in him is no darkness
at all"* (1 Jn. 1:5). It is the height of folly to think that
there will be two scales, and if the good one has done in
life outweighs the bad, all will go well. The God of the
universe is no shimmering, foundationless bowl of jelly
to be slithered about and shaped by the wishes of men.
And what of His boundless love? It must ever be remembered that men cannot choose and pick among God's
attributes, accepting those they like and rejecting those
which are offensive to them. The same God who is a God
of love is a God of absolute holiness. And what His holiness condemns, His love can never embrace. The divine
perfections are not "unequally" yoked together.

The Judge at the Great White Throne is the Lord Jesus Christ, and the basis of the judgment can be expressed in four words. Men will be judged ". . . *according to their works*" (Rev. 20:12, 13). The contrast is striking. Those who come to Christ at Calvary acknowledge, "Nothing in my hand I bring, simply to the cross I cling." At the Great White Throne, they take the attitude expressed in the poem "Invictus": "I am the master of my fate. I am the captain of my soul." How absolutely ludicrous for a man to think that he can live successfully, or live at all, apart from the One who is the source of all life.

Still, with pride of heart, those who are found standing before the Judge will have presumed that through self-effort they can satisfy the demands of an infinitely holy God.

If the Judge is the Lord Jesus Christ, and if the basis of the judgment is ". . . *according to their works*", there remains one further question. What is the judgment that will be inflicted?

This is the twentieth century. It is the most enlightened period of all of human history. More scientific progress has been made in the last seventy-five years than all the accumulated advances of the previous centuries combined. Hydrogen bombs, men on the moon, heart transplants, computer technology — these and other "advances" have dramatically and spasmodically altered the course of life. At such a moment in history, can an informed, intelligent human being believe in a literal hell — a place of conscious eternal torment — of separation from God? Not only should he, but if he doesn't, it is because he is shackled in the chains of pride. In everything in life, men are faced with alternatives — love and hate, peace and war, hot and cold, yes and no, up and down, fast and slow, wide and narrow, light and dark —

life and death, Heaven and hell. The Apostle John wrote, *"And whosoever was not found written in the book of life was cast into the lake of fire"* (Rev. 20:15). And, if this truth offends the sensitivities of some men, the problem is to be found not in God's justice, but in man's ignorance of it. For finite, mortal man has no right to find fault with his infinite, immortal Creator.

At the Great White Throne, the Judge will be the Lord Jesus Christ; the basis of the judgment, *". . . according to their works";* and the judgment itself will be consignment to eternal torment.

Directness is required here — there is far too much at stake. Have you been to Calvary to meet the loving, gracious Lamb who has provided for glorious, unending life — or are you going to appear at the Great White Throne where you will meet the infinitely holy and just Lion who will decree unending torment? Have you settled your case out of court? The Lord of eternity sends no man to Heaven or hell. Created in the image of God, with responsibility to choose, each man makes that decision for himself. Calvary and life — or the Great White Throne and death.

The second is the stellar heaven. This is the sphere of the heavenly bodies — the sun, moon and stars. To this sphere science has propelled astronauts and cosmonauts. But beyond, man uninvited cannot go.

15

Heaven's for Real

The old spiritual, "Everybody talkin' 'bout Heaven ain't goin' there" presents accurate biblical truth. *". . . for wide is the gate, and broad is the way, that leadeth to destruction, and many there be who go in that way; Because narrow is the gate, and hard is the way, which leadeth unto life, and few there be that find it"* (Mt. 7:13-14). Here is the classic example of the principle that the majority is not always right. With the eternal destiny of the soul itself in the balance, most of humanity down through the ages has taken the wrong fork in the road. It has always been only a remnant that has had a heart for God. Therefore, when the ungodly reject the reality of Heaven — when they vent displeasure at the expression of a literal hell — the true believer should be neither surprised, dismayed nor discouraged.

A test tube can neither prove nor disprove the reality of Heaven. Empiricism, pragmatism and sense perception provide no solution. Admittedly, both the believer and the unbeliever accept their respective views by 'faith'. But, if the unbeliever is one day proven to be wrong — if there is a Heaven, and he did not prepare for it — he will have lost everything — a price beyond measure to pay for his mistake. If (speaking hypothetically), on the other hand, the believer is one day proven to be wrong — if, perchance, there is no Heaven, no God, no life after death — he will still have lived a good life and lost nothing. It is the unbeliever, therefore, who must exercise the greater 'faith', and that on the flimsiest and most contradictory of evidence. In the final analysis, men reject God, creationism and Heaven because of pride. For, if God exists, then man is responsible to this higher Being. If man chooses to reject that obligation, the only alternative is to postulate evolution, no matter how illogical and fraught with problems. But, God does exist, and Heaven is real. And man must one day give an account to his Creator.

But where is Heaven? And what is it like? Can we take a peek beyond the clouds of life? One of the commonly used words for Heaven in the Hebrew Old Testament is the word "Shamayim". It literally means "high" or "lofty", and in actuality, there are three heavens. The first is the atmospheric heaven. This is the sphere immediately surrounding the crust of the earth. Here the fowl of the air spread their wings and soar.

The second is the stellar heaven. This is the sphere of the heavenly bodies — the sun, moon and stars. To this sphere science has propelled astronauts and cosmonauts. But beyond, man uninvited cannot go.

Finally, the Bible refers to the *"third heaven"* (2 Cor. 12:2, 4). This is the domain of God. And with reference to earth, Heaven is always up. Here the redeemed of all ages will know peace and joy unspeakable with the One who is the source of all life.

While God has not seen fit to reveal details concerning what the *"third heaven"* will be like, some facts can be gleaned from the biblical narrative. First, Heaven is **permanent**. The Apostle Paul, writing to believers in Corinth, reminded them that *". . . if our earthly house of this tabernacle were dissolved, we have a building of God, an house not made with hands, eternal in the heavens"* (2 Cor. 5:1). Simply stated, Paul was saying that when this physical, mortal body returns to the dust from which it came, the believer has a spiritual, immortal body that will never know pain, decay or death.

Second, Heaven is **preferred.** How strange that sounds to the ear. Men cling tenaciously to life; they try desperately not to let go – to somehow find the fountain of youth. Little do they understand that death for the believer is swallowed up in victory. It has lost its sting (1 Cor. 15:55). Why then retreat with fear from cancer, or heart attack, or accident, or any of a myriad of other causes of death? Ah, you say, it is not a fear of death but of dying. How foolish! If you are an heir of the King, do you suppose that the God who has loved you with an everlasting love, who has redeemed you by His blood, who is building a mansion for you far beyond anything this world has ever known, will not provide the comfort of His abiding presence and grace sufficient for that hour?

Hear the example of the great Apostle Paul: *". . . having a desire* [he said] *to depart and to be with Christ* [through death], *which is far better. Nevertheless, to abide in the flesh is more needful for you"* (Phil. 1:23-24. Listen to the Apostle once again: *"For to me to live is Christ, and to die is gain"* (Phil. 1:21). It is not only what was said, but the one who said it, which makes these statements so significant. In his letter to the Corinthians, Paul tells of a man who was caught up to the *"third heaven";* whether in the body or out of the body he did not know. That is, Paul did not know if the man was alive or not. What was known was that while in the third heaven, that man heard unspeakable words that were so glorious they were not permitted to be uttered on earth (2 Cor. 12:4). That man was Paul, himself, stoned at Lystra and left for dead (Acts 14:19-20). He was one of the few men in history to be given a glimpse of Heaven and permitted to remain here on earth.

It was this same man who said Heaven is preferred. *". . . having a desire to depart and to be with Christ, which is far better. . ."* (Phil. 1:23). Stretch the "far" as far as your mind will take you, and you will not have begun to exhaust how far better Heaven is to earth. Therefore, it is preferred.

Third and finally, Heaven is **perfect**. The description given in the twenty-first chapter of Revelation is striking. There is an absolute absence of negatives. John put it this way: *"And God shall wipe away all tears from their eyes; and there shall be NO more death, NEITHER sorrow, NOR crying, NEITHER shall there be any more pain; for the former things are passed away"* (Rev. 21:4). And there will be NO need for light because, *". . . the Lord God giveth them light. . ."* (Rev. 22:5).

Dear reader, Heaven is **permanent**. Heaven is **preferred**. Heaven is **perfect**. If you are a citizen of Heaven, look up for your glorious redemption draweth nigh. If you are not, look out, for judgment is coming just as surely as night follows day. But, there is still time to flee to safety in the outstretched, waiting arms of Jesus.

The poet aptly described God's attitude toward you this way:

> *The love of God is greater far*
> *Than tongue or pen can ever tell;*
> *It goes beyond the highest star,*
> *And reaches to the lowest hell.*
> *The guilty pair, bowed down with care,*
> *God gave His Son to win;*
> *His erring child He reconciled,*
> *And pardoned from his sin,*
>
> *When hoary time shall pass away,*
> *And earthly thrones and kingdoms fall;*
> *When men who here refuse to pray,*

On rocks and hills and mountains call;
God's love, so sure, shall still endure,
All measureless and strong;
Redeeming grace to Adam's race —
The saints' and angels' song.

Could we with ink the ocean fill,
And were the skies of parchment made;
Were ev'ry stalk on earth a quill,
And ev'ry man a scribe by trade;
To write the love of God above
Would drain the ocean dry;
Nor could the scroll contain the whole,
Tho' stretched from sky to sky.

Oh, love of God, how rich and pure!
How measureless and strong!
It shall forevermore endure —
The saints' and angels' song.

And the Spirit and the bride say, Come. And
let him that heareth say, Come. And let him
that is athirst come. And whosoever will, let
him take the water of life freely.
                        Revelation 22:17

Man was created to glorify God and that is accomplished as he allows his life to be an instrument through which the intrinsic, eternal perfection of God is displayed.

16

Postscript:
The Glory of God

"Why was I born? Why am I living? What have I got? What am I giving?" These questions are not new – men have asked them since time immemorial. What is life and living really all about? Is there rhyme and rhythm, meaning and purpose in existing? Or, is life simply the rotating of the roulette wheel? Round and round it goes – but where it stops, nobody knows. Must man play the hand he is dealt? Is life, after all, simply blind fatalism?

To such questions, many theologians have a ready answer: "The chief end of man is to glorify God." And with this, the Scriptures agree: *"For of him, and through him, and to him, are all things: to whom be glory forever. Amen"* (Rom. 11:36). But what IS the glory of God? The psalmist said, *"The heavens declare the glory of God. . . "* (Ps. 19:1). Fine, but what is it that the heavens are declaring? Both angels and ascended saints proclaim, *"Thou art worthy, O Lord, to receive glory and honor and power. . . "* (Rev. 4:11). But what is it that God is receiving? What IS the glory of God? It seems reasonable to assume that if the purpose for man's creation is to glorify God (and it is), then the understanding of that glory should be mankind's highest intellectual pursuit, and its outworking his greatest priority. In light of that, it seems strange that so little is said about the glory of God. No theme is loftier and no subject more directly related to your life.

A recently taken poll of friends, pastors, Bible teachers and church congregations showed little agreement and only a vague understanding on the subject of "The Glory of God." Some suggested that God received glory through the saving of souls; others made reference to the Shekinah glory of God mentioned in the Old Testament; still others quoted verses that made reference to the glory of God but could not define what it is. A few thought that the glory of God related in some way to the holiness of God. All were inadequate answers. A major theological reference book gave this definition: "God's glory is that which makes Him glorious." But that doesn't help much. You can't properly define a word by using the word in the definition.

Again, the question is asked: Since man was created for God's glory, what IS the glory of God? Here is a working definition: God's glory is the sum and substance of His intrinsic, eternal perfection. "Intrinsic" underscores the fact that God's glory emanates wholly from within His own being. That is, it is not dependent upon anything external to Himself. "Eternal" emphasizes the longevity of God's glory — there was never an instant in the past, nor will there be in the future, when the universe is without God's glory. "Perfection" refers to both the qualitative and quantitative ingredients that compose the divine Being. These include His existence, essence, personality, sovereignty, decree and attributes. Large words, these — but take a closer look at them.

The divine
EXISTENCE —   **God is.**

The divine
ESSENCE —   **God is one spiritual Being in three Persons.**

The divine PERSONALITY –	God is one spiritual Being in three Persons **possessing intellect, emotion and will.**
The divine SOVEREIGNTY –	God is one spiritual Being in three Persons possessing intellect, emotion and will, **who does things according to His own good pleasure.**
The divine DECREE –	God is one spiritual Being in three Persons possessing intellect, emotion and will, who does things according to His own good pleasure, **and therefore originates and executes, either actively or permissively, all that comes to pass.**
The divine ATTRIBUTES	God is one spiritual Being in three Persons possessing intellect, emotion and will, who does things according to His own good pleasure, and therefore originates and executes, either actively or permissively, all that comes to pass **in perfect harmony with His own character.**

The character of God is theologically referred to as God's attributes. These are innate qualities which are "attributed" to God. These divine attributes can only be known to their fullest extent through God's self-disclosure in the Bible. On the basis of that revelation, it can be said that God is infinite, eternal, unchangeable, all-present, all-knowing, all-powerful, righteous, just, loving, good and faithful. God must always function in perfect harmony with His attributes, since He never changes.

While God's glory is intrinsic because it belongs to Him like light and heat belong to the sun, **it is the divine plan that His glory be both proclaimed and demonstrated on the stage of the planet Earth through the outworking of human history.** Not by man — because he can neither add to nor diminish from an infinite Creator — but through the instrumentation of man, God is making His glory known.

It should not be inferred that because the glory of God is the pinnacle and consummation of all things, that God is himself self-seeking or self-centered. Rather, since God by his very nature seeks the highest and best, and since He IS the highest and best, He must bring all things to completion in Himself (Rom. 11:36).

Man was created to glorify God and that is accomplished as he allows his life to be an instrument through which the intrinsic, eternal perfection of God is displayed. In light of this truth, the fundamental problem of mankind, from which all else springs, can be summed up quite easily. Social scientists inform us that the most often used word in the English language is "I". It should be "Him". Man is self-centered instead of God-centered. His frame of reference is all wrong. His philosophy, his values, his deeds are all directed toward self-gratification and contrary to his Creator and the purpose for which he was created.

It was God who breathed into man the breath of life, and man became a living soul. For those from among humanity who know and submit to the will of God, there is perfect peace, joy unspeakable and highest destiny. For those who reject the will of God, there is only distress and eternal anguish.

But now, back to an earlier quotation: *"The heavens declare the glory of God. . . ."* In what way do the heavens declare God's glory? First, they reveal His existence — creation requires a Creator. Second, they reveal His wisdom — design requires a Designer. Third, they reveal His power — movement requires a Mover. And fourth, if, as some scientists suggest, the universe is endless, the heavens reveal His infinity.

The gaze of man, however, should be centered not so much on the heavens above — but on the earth below. For on this planet, the fullest reflection of the glory of God is to be seen. The heavens may reveal His existence, wisdom, power and infinity — but His holiness, justice, love, mercy, goodness and faithfulness are proclaimed and experienced on earth.

It was the holiness of God from which Adam and Eve fled after sinning in the Garden of Eden (Gen. 3:8). And in the clothing of the first couple in the skin of animals, the justice of God was exhibited (Gen. 3:21). Blood had to be shed — one had to take the place of another — punishment had to be meted out. God could only forgive sin on the basis of His justice. The entrance of sin through the permissive will of God and man's direct disobedience was essential if certain of the divine attributes, such as holiness, justice and mercy, were to be displayed.

Moses was about to climb Mount Sinai for the second time. He needed a fresh glimpse of God — a renewing in the inward man. He requested, *"Now therefore, I pray thee, if I have found grace in thy sight, show me now thy way, that I may know thee, that I may find grace in thy sight. . ."* (Ex. 33:13). Moses wanted to know what God was like. He continued, *". . . I beseech thee, show me thy glory"* (Ex. 33:18). God told Moses that no man could look on His face and live — to view the fullness of His glory, which included holiness, would mean certain death. But, God placed His servant in the cleft of the rock — He would pass by and let Moses see His back, His nonconsuming attributes of mercy, grace, longsuffering, goodness and truth (Ex. 34:6). Moses needed no more incentive. He would descend from the mount with the reflection of the glory of God on his face, ready for the task ahead (Ex. 34:29).

God chose to manifest His glory to Israel in the Tabernacle in the wilderness, and later in the Temple at Jerusalem. This was a self-disclosure of His presence and perfection among His people (Ex. 40:34; 1 Ki. 8:11).

In time, the age of law gave way to the age of grace. The Old Covenant gave way to the New Covenant. A people were called into being called the Church, the body of Christ. Indwelt by the Holy Spirit, the believer is in a unique position to be a vessel fit for the Master's use. Attributes of God such as grace, mercy, love, holiness, justice and omnipotence were demonstrated at the place called Calvary and are discernible in the lives of true heirs of God's redemption.

The glory of God has been revealed in creation, in the Garden of Eden, on the face of Moses in connection with the giving of the law, in the Tabernacle, in the Temple and in the life of the believer. But, only the descendants of Abraham, Isaac and Jacob are called by God, "My Glory". He declared, *". . . I will place salvation in Zion for Israel, my glory"* (Isa. 46:13). **The fullest reflection of the intrinsic, eternal perfection of God is to be seen in His relationship with Israel, not in degree but in comprehensiveness.** The world has little understood this fundamental truth. God's existence, essence, personality, sovereignty, decree and attributes are showcased most completely in the election, dispersion, preservation and future restoration and glorification of- His chosen people.

Every spiritual blessing which the Church possesses is provided for within the framework of the New Covenant which God made with Israel (Jer. 31:31-40) and which the Lord instituted in the Upper Room only hours before His crucifixion (Mt. 26:26-29).

There is, however, one further way whereby God's glory is preeminently seen. The beloved Apostle John wrote, ". . . *the Word was made flesh, and dwelt among us, and we beheld his glory. . .* " (Jn. 1:14). Of course, he was referring to Jesus Christ, the Son of God. In this same vein, the Apostle Peter said, *"For we have not followed cunningly devised fables when we made known unto you the power and coming of our Lord Jesus Christ, but were eyewitnesses of his majesty"* (2 Pet. 1:16). Both John and Peter were speaking of the occasion when they were with Jesus on the Mount of Transfiguration, and His eternal glory shone out of His humanity (Mt. 17:2). The writer to the Hebrews, speaking of Christ's unsurpassing glory, said that He was the very effulgence (brightness of the glory) of the Father. That is, unlike other manifestations of God's glory which were mirror-like reflections, Christ was the exact reality and substance of that glory, for Jesus was God in flesh (Heb. 1:3). For that reason, He could say, ". . . *He that hath seen me hath seen the Father. . .* " (Jn. 14:9). And again, *"I and my Father are one"* (Jn. 10:30).

How, then, should the child of God respond to the paramount truth of his Father's glory?

First, he should respond as did the Prophet Isaiah who, when confronted with the glory of God, cried out,

*". . . Woe is me! For I am undone, because I am a man
of unclean lips, and I dwell in the midst of a people of
unclean lips; for mine eyes have seen the King, the Lord
of hosts"* (Isa. 6:5). Men only see themselves as they
are when they first see God as He is. The intrinsic, eternal perfection of God (His glory) is the only platinum
yardstick by which to measure life. Here is the absolute
standard by which every thought and deed may be ap-
praised.

If a man, in his relationship with his wife, fulfilled the
purpose for which he was created, he would proclaim
and demonstrate God's intrinsic, eternal perfection. He
would be holy, just, loving, good, merciful and longsuffering toward his mate.

In raising a child, conducting business, international
relations, the same principle would apply. In other words,
if men fulfilled the purpose for which they were created,
the earth would be a paradise. "Ah," someone says, 'if
others did it to me, I would do it back. If my husband
were good to me, I would be good to him. If he were longsuffering with my shortcomings, I would be with his."
But, that's exactly the point. God created man to reflect His glory, no matter how others may respond. It
is the exact opposite of "I'll scratch your back if you
scratch mine." God loved you while you were unlovely,
alienated and an enemy. It was because of that love that
He died for you. How you respond has nothing to do
with His action.

Second, he should purpose in his heart to fulfill the
design for which he was created. The Apostle Paul identified that purpose succinctly when he wrote, *"Whether,
therefore, ye eat, or drink, or whatever ye do, do all to
the glory of God"* (1 Cor. 10:31). And again, *"For to me
to live is Christ* [that is, by word and deed, to show
forth His glory], *and to die is gain"* (Phil. 1:21).

Third, he must obey divine priorities. Since the chief end of man is to glorify God, the chief end of man cannot be to win souls. They are not synonymous. The latter is only one of many streams that flow out of the former. The pastor who preaches fifty-two varieties of "John 3:16" each year may win converts, but he is not making disciples. He is guilty of dual error. He is not fulfilling one of the purposes for which God has called him (to preach the whole counsel of God, Acts 20:27), nor is he feeding the sheep entrusted to his care. Every week, millions of people with hurting hearts wend their way to church, hoping to hear the Word of the Lord from a man sent by God. They rightfully expect to hear a man who speaks with authority from a hot heart, because it has been touched with coals from off the altar in the divine presence. All too often, what is heard is the voice of a man with little authority and even less fervor. The harried pastor has spent his time and energy on lesser matters because his priorities are out of sequence. And, multitudes leave the "house" of the Lord with the same hurting hearts with which they entered, not having been exposed to new glimpses of the divine glory.

Fourth and finally, the child of God should fall prostrate before the divine wisdom, remembering that, *". . . my thoughts are not your thoughts, neither are your ways my ways, saith the Lord. For as the heavens are higher than the earth, so are my ways higher than your ways, and my thoughts higher than your thoughts"* (Isa. 55:8-9).

The Bible teaches that unregenerate man is an enemy of God and under divine condemnation (Rom. 1:1 - 3:19). By grace through faith in Christ's redemptive work on Calvary, he is justified (Rom. 3:20 - 5:21). As he yields to the indwelling Holy Spirit, he is being sanctified (Rom. 6:1 - 8:27). And one day he is going to be glorified (Rom. 8:28-30). God never leaves things half done. What He begins, He finishes. He begins with a condemned man — molds and shapes him, until he is one day conformed to the glory of God. He takes a man who was an enemy and makes him an exalted, eternal son. The Apostle Paul put it this way, ". . . *whom he did predestinate, them he also called; and whom he called, them he also justified; and whom he justified, them he also glorified"* (Rom. 8:30).

When God completes His work in and through His redeemed child, that child will reflect fully and perfectly his Father's intrinsic, eternal glory. It is in this potential that the dignity, nobility and worth of man is to be seen. Jude, the half-brother of the Lord, summed it up this way: *"Now unto him that is able to keep you from falling, and to present you faultless before the presence of his glory with exceeding joy, to the only wise God, our Savior, be glory and majesty, dominion and power, both now and ever. Amen"* (Jude 24-25).

What fathomless grace is this!